N E E D H A M
FREE PUBLIC
L I B R A R Y

Given by

Ann C. MacFate

In Memory of

Betty Ann Keane

Praise for
MIDNIGHT LULLABIES

"This is a book I wish I had seven years ago as I cradled my first baby. It wraps up all of the big, and sometimes scary emotions of motherhood in truth. It silences lies, some that we didn't even know we were telling ourselves. Proverbs 12:20 tells us that "Those who plan peace have joy," and each chapter of this book is a strategic step in that Peace Plan. Lauren sheds light on many of the subjects I grapple with regularly as a mom, as well as some areas that I did not know I was neglecting. In grace, she provides simple yet powerful next steps to be taken toward a more peace-filled mamahood. This is a book I will be gifting to many mama friends, and it is one I will be revisiting myself throughout the many stages of motherhood."

—Eryn Lynum, speaker and author of *936 Pennies: Discovering the Joy of Intentional Parenting*

"Lauren is an unparalleled prayer warrior. And for someone like me, who struggles to even remember to pray—let alone do so coherently—her easy, breezy way of talking to God is a welcome source of light inside a dark and consuming cave. Lauren's devotional offers up actionable steps for wrangling the wild, unruly emotions of motherhood—as well as a daily dose of hope-fueled encouragement designed to help us release our self-imposed shame and grab hold of our sustaining 'even though.' This book belongs on nightstands everywhere. There won't be a copy without dog-eared corners, a cracked spine, and beautiful stains of hot tears of relief over Lauren's life-giving words."

—Jodie Utter, writer and blogger at Utter Imperfection

"Lauren's vulnerability and relatability are unmatched. Women will close *Midnight Lullabies* feeling understood, encouraged, comforted, and pointed north to the one who calls them worthy even when they feel anything but." —Jillian Benfield, special needs mom, owner of JillianBenfield.com

"Lauren's words need to be read by women in the trenches of motherhood. You'll cry, you'll smile, you will relate to every beautiful mess found between these pages.

"Mothers are busy and we don't make enough time to find God in our everyday lives. But you can find Him in *Midnight Lullabies*. The daily chapters walk you through the muck of those tough years when our kids are young and our marriages are pushed to their limits.

"And if you get distracted by a crying baby or a hungry husband, you can put the book down and pick it back up, right where you left it, with ease.

"There aren't enough women telling the world to love our husbands (yes, even when they make us mad), to love ourselves (yes, even when we doubt), and most of all, to love God. Lauren does that. You'll love *Midnight Lullabies*. You'll love Lauren Eberspacher. We all do."

—Leslie Means, founder and owner of
Her View From Home

"The authentic and heartfelt writings of *Midnight Lullabies* met me in motherhood with the truth and hope that my weary soul needed. Lauren's words bring biblical truth to every mother and make you feel like you're sitting with a friend over coffee. You can feel Lauren's soul in her writing, and I can always count on her words for encouragement."

—Caitlin Henderson, Faith, Farming, and Family

"I have been in love with Lauren's beautiful, faith-filled writing for years. And *Midnight Lullabies* was no exception. Her message always comes from a place of genuine, honest love for the Lord and her readers. When *Midnight Lullabies* became part of my morning devotion, I started every day with tears in my eyes, peace in my heart, and a new outlook on how to overcome the challenges of motherhood."

—Terryn Drieling, Faith Family & Beef

"As the director of Mom's Connection, a faith based group for mothers, I believe *Midnight Lullabies* is a much-needed resource and devotional for moms. Moms need daily encouragement, but are often over looked as they go about meeting the needs of everyone else in the family. Lauren has done a wonderful job of exploring so thoughtfully the different issues moms face while offering great hope! The 'one step into' part of each devotional helps women put application to what's been shared, which is a crucial step in anyone's faith walk."

—Sherry White, The Messy Christian blog

"Lauren's servant heart shines as brightly as the stars in the pages of *Midnight Lullabies*. Lauren shares openly, honestly, and with refreshing relatability about both the deep challenge and immense joy of motherhood. Her words are rooted in truth, and steeped in the hope of Christ. A must-have for busy moms who are yearning for moments of peace in the midst of motherhood."

—Carolyn Moore, editor, Her View
from Home

"*Midnight Lullabies* champions a mama's heart and soothes a mama's soul. Lauren has a way of reaching her hand out through the words she's penned to grasp the hand of the woman reading them. She offers camaraderie in the loneliness and understanding in the trenches of motherhood, while helping mamas navigate their emotions with the truth of God's word. Lauren's empathetic nature embraces a mama's soul, allowing her to feel heard and understood in her struggles, while also sharing practical steps to help her traverse the struggle and claim God's peace. More than anything, *Midnight Lullabies* shares not only encouragement for the day, but hope for eternity through the love and grace we find in Jesus Christ."

—Ginger Hughes, author of the No
Mama's Perfect blog

"Motherhood can be a lonely endeavor and no woman should have to do it alone. In *Midnight Lullabies* Lauren becomes the friend, the witness, and the inspiration to mothers everywhere who are struggling in the trenches." —Liz Petrone, writer at lizpetrone.com and author of the upcoming book *The Price of Admission*

"Lauren Eberspacher's writing is consistently relatable, meaningful, and uplifting. Whether she's tackling topics like post-pregnancy weight gain, post-kid date nights, or postpartum depression, Lauren gives voice to the true thoughts percolating in other moms' subconscious (but exhausted!) minds. Even better, she helps her fellow moms feel more grounded and less alone." —Laura Coffey, editor of the *TODAY* show's Parenting Team community and bestselling author of *My Old Dog: Rescued Pets with Remarkable Second Acts*

"As a mental health professional and older mother of two stepchildren, I am always seeking to read stories and articles that lift me and enlighten me and reach my Mom soul. That's where the beautiful writer Lauren Eberspacher enters the picture. She writes with such exquisite honesty and genuineness that it is impossible not to be affected by her words. I walk away from reading her posts with a more compassionate and tolerant view of the world around me. Her spirit is contagious and you FEEL her when she writes. You almost come to believe that she is in your living room speaking directly to you. That's a gift that you rarely encounter among the most masterful of writers. Her words stay with you long after you are through and you sense that she has empowered you to think bigger and better and beyond yourself. There's a magic in how she gets you to listen, and the most important piece of this magic is that you are made to feel like you matter and that you are never really alone. If I had to choose one writer to read each and every day exclusively, it would without any doubt be Lauren Eberspacher, who in being herself has managed to shape the minds of thousands of women everywhere, and I am one of them. She has a devoted lifelong fan in me!" —Lisa Leshaw, MS CMHC, leader of women's counseling groups, writer for *Chicken Soup for the Soul* and *Huffington Post*

"As Lauren Eberspacher's pastor, I have had the privilege of getting to know her in the full spectrum of ministry, personal, and family settings. She is a passionate pursuer of God's truth and has a winsome way of articulating it as she writes with authenticity about the ordinary—and not so ordinary—experiences of everyday life. She also writes with the unusual combination of vulnerability and transparency coupled with wisdom beyond her years that leaves you wanting more. I have the highest confidence in the quality of Lauren's spiritual counsel, which you will find seamlessly folded in with a good dose of tears and giggles."

—Jim Hight, D Min, lead pastor of Beth-El
Community Church, Milford, NE

"I have had the joy of watching Lauren mature and thrive in her role as wife and mother and have appreciated hearing her heart through her blog. Lauren's love for the Lord and desire to encourage young moms by sharing her real-life ups and downs comes through in her authentic writing. Her writing not only brings much-needed reassurance of God's presence through this season of life, but she also inspires all women's hearts to lean in and grasp the fullness of God's love. I pray that this devotional will encourage all of us to embrace how wide, how long, how high, and how deep His love is, and may He strengthen those whose hearts belong to Him."

—Cindy Bentele, Bible-leading teacher and children's
director for international ministry

"Lauren's words are like a salve for the soul. Her raw honesty and vulnerability paint a realistic picture of motherhood that every woman can benefit from hearing.

"*Midnight Lullabies* walks you through a hard-fought battle to tap into the grace and mercy that only a loving God can provide. Lauren bravely shares from the depths of a mother's post-partum journey, chronicling her painfully relatable road from the pit to the mountaintop.

"Mamas, friends, you need these words. Read them, study them, and allow them to nourish your spirit."

—Brynn Burger, The Mama on the Rocks

MIDNIGHT LULLABIES

Moments of Peace for Moms

Lauren Eberspacher

NASHVILLE NEW YORK

FaithWords
Hachette Book Group
1290 Avenue of the Americas, New York, NY 10104
faithwords.com
twitter.com/faithwords
First Edition: April 2019

FaithWords is a division of Hachette Book Group, Inc. The FaithWords name and logo are trademarks of Hachette Book Group, Inc.

The publisher is not responsible for websites (or their content) that are not owned by the publisher.

The Hachette Speakers Bureau provides a wide range of authors for speaking events. To find out more, go to www.hachettespeakersbureau.com or call (866) 376-6591.

LCCN: 2018964673

ISBNs: 978-1-5460-3519-0 (hardcover), 978-1-5460-3520-6 (ebook)

Printed in the United States of America

LSC-C

10 9 8 7 6 5 4 3 2 1

For Eric,

The half that makes me whole, the other pea in my pod, and my very best friend. Thank you for always pushing me closer to Jesus and loving me so well. I adore you.

For Nora, Andi, and Deacon,

You are my most treasured little gifts. It is my greatest honor to be your mommy and the one who gets to sing you your midnight lullabies. May you chase after Jesus, always.

CONTENTS

Your Invitation   xiii

Day 1   The Stand to Become More and the Lie of
the Big-Girl Panties   1

Day 2   When the Enemy Tells You That You're
Not Enough   6

Day 3   When You Bring a Sacred Offering   10

Day 4   When You Believe the Lie of Loneliness   15

Day 5   But What Happens When You Still Want a Friend?   20

Day 6   When Your Expectations Aren't Met   24

Day 7   When Our Sex Life Meets Our Prayer Life   29

Day 8   When Mama Gets Angry   33

Day 9   When You're Asked to Make Another
Dozen Cookies   37

Day 10   When Mama Needs Wisdom   42

Day 11   When Anger Becomes Resentment   46

Day 12   When Your Mom Bod Becomes Your Idol   51

Day 13   When Comparison Sticks Its Foot in the Door   55

Day 14   When Mama Gets Her Joy Back   61

Day 15   When Mom Fear Is Consuming   66

Day 16   When Jesus Commands Us to Go   72

Day 17	When You Find Yourself in Seasons of Sacrifice	77
Day 18	When Pride Keeps You from Opening the Door	82
Day 19	When You're Asked to Pay a Price	87
Day 20	When It's Time to Put Down the Mop	92
Day 21	When You Feel Defeated at Church	96
Day 22	When Mama Gets Her Feelings Hurt	101
Day 23	When You're Given the Choice to Get In	105
Day 24	When Motherhood Becomes Your Gift	109
Day 25	When You Forget How to Be a Bride	113
Day 26	When Mama Gets Sick	118
Day 27	When You Parent with Shame	122
Day 28	When You Believe Who Regret Says You Are	127
Day 29	When Mama Sets the Example	131
Day 30	When God Lets You Walk into the Fire	136
Day 31	When Motherhood Is Redeemed	143
	Acknowledgments	149
	Index	153
	About the Author	159

YOUR INVITATION

I sat in a heap on my bed, my hair in a messy bun; the baby was playing down on the floor. There was laundry scattered all over the room, some of it clean, some of it dirty. But if I'm being really honest, I was too over it to care.

I was six months into motherhood and felt like I was sinking beneath the weight of it all and wondering where God was in the middle of it. The high of the newborn stage had worn off and the exhaustion of mom life had set in. The reality that I wasn't who I once was had hit me like a ton of bricks, and I realized that I couldn't just keep trying to tread these uncharted waters any longer.

Not only was I unable to contend with the housework, but I couldn't keep up with the emotions that were overpowering my mind, either. And oh, I had so many emotions: feelings that felt so big and so raw, feelings that I was defenseless against. And the enemy knew it.

I had tried to work through them on my own, and for a while I really believed I was beginning to make some progress. But just when I thought I was starting to see the fog lift, all of the other emotions would come tumbling down around me like a chain reaction. It made it difficult for me to do even the simplest of things, let alone enjoy doing them. Whether it was the middle of the day or the middle of the night, my emotions ruled my life and affected everything in it.

I was stuck in an emotional identity crisis of motherhood with absolutely no idea of how I was going to get out.

I think the thing that can be so confusing about our emotions is that they are instantaneous; our minds can go from zero to one hundred in a second. And if the emotion is strong enough for long enough, that feeling becomes our source of truth, and we get trapped into believing the lies that our emotions make us feel. Oftentimes, this feeling of being trapped leads us to making decisions and believing things about ourselves and God that we wouldn't think to be true otherwise. And when we act on these feelings in a moment of heightened emotion, there are always repercussions, and it almost always ends up with my peace disappearing and my motherhood stolen.

Here's the thing about emotions, friend. My emotions are indicators, not dictators. My emotions are not my source of truth.

But God is. And in a world that tells us to "follow your heart" and "do what feels good," we must stand up to the lies that our emotions are going to try to tell us and look to what is completely stable instead. And that's God's Word.

God created us to experience emotions. He even allows us to feel the bad ones. But that doesn't mean he wants us to stay stuck in them. And choosing to remain in bondage to these emotions will only leave you and me with an unsettled heart and a constant yearning for peace that seems so very far out of our reach. And it's so tiring to keep reaching for something that seems so far away, isn't it?

I don't know about you, but it's hard to know how to step

back into that place of peace in motherhood. It's overwhelming to think what I need to do first to get to a mindset where my vision is clear and my emotions aren't owning me. It's hard to act when you feel so stuck.

But together, this month, we are going to break through the darkness of our emotions and step back into the light of God's peace. It isn't going to be easy. In fact, it's going to hurt. But what we are going to find is that our emotions in light of the love of God and who he says we are changes everything. And when you are given the opportunity to take that step back into his peace, back into the design for who he created for you to be as a mom, you can take that step in confidence, trusting that God is leading you back where he longs for you to be. *In his perfect peace.*

Do you find yourself sitting on your bed like I was that day, friend? Are you tired of being stuck in the chaos of your emotions? Are ready to break free of the chains enslaving you? What if you stood up against the lies of the enemy and refused to be a slave to them any longer, but became the woman God designed you to be and have your motherhood redeemed? Are you ready to take a stand?

A stand against:

The loneliness.

The lack of confidence.

The insecurity.

The anger.

The sadness.

The doubt.

The anxiety.

The exhaustion.

The envy.

The things that keep you up at night that you can't stand to hang on to a moment longer.

It is time to reclaim our emotions, hand them back over to the One who created us to experience them, and renew our minds in the freedom of Christ. Are you ready?

> *You keep him in perfect peace*
> *whose mind is stayed on you,*
> *because he trusts in you.*
> *Trust in the LORD forever,*
> *for the LORD GOD is an everlasting rock.*
>
> ISAIAH 26:3–4

Day 1

THE STAND TO BECOME MORE AND THE LIE OF THE BIG-GIRL PANTIES

For freedom Christ has set us free; stand firm therefore, and do not submit again to a yoke of slavery.

GALATIANS 5:1

They laid that baby on my chest, and everything changed. Half of my husband, half of me, and a part of my heart that I never knew was there was instantly overflowing with love.

Fierce, unwavering, terrifying love.

In an instant, the love of this babe changed my heart. And in those moments, everything was perfect, and I found myself wondering how I ever lived a day of my life without her. In those moments, everything was just as they told me it would be.

But nobody told me just how fast it could all change or how broken I could become.

When I was pregnant with our first daughter, I remember being given more than enough advice from other mamas. Because it's the duty of those of us who have gone before to pass the gift of this knowledge on, right? Women would sit me down at church and take me by the hands, telling me how happy this next chapter of my life was going to be. Ladies sat around at my baby shower as we *oohed* and *ahhed* over teeny-tiny baby clothes and told me to savor every moment of their littleness. Even the random woman at the grocery store felt it her job to tell me about the overwhelmingly beautiful experience that I was about to partake in.

But nobody told me.

Nobody told me that the emotions of motherhood could make me become completely undone. Nobody told me in the midst of the happiest days of my life and in the songs of the midnight lullabies I would sing in my daughter's nursery that I would find myself on my knees, trapped in the fury of my emotions and wondering who I had become and where the woman I once was had gone. Everyone had failed to mention that Satan was on the prowl to steal my motherhood and that he would start with the rawest emotions of my heart to do it.

One of the costliest pieces of advice that I was given by these well-meaning women was that of the big-girl panties. They talked about them like they were a prize to be worn, a trophy of strength and resilience. It's based on the belief that mothers must not give in to the frailty of their own hearts; when one pulls up the big-girl panties, they simultaneously push down all of the emotions. For most, it is the battle cry of motherhood. But the big-girl panties came at a price, one that I, like most women, was willing to pay. And that's the price of vulnerability. Not just with everyone else, but with ourselves and our unwillingness to let God into the sacred space of it, either.

This pushing down of our emotions, this compartmentalization of our very souls, is one of the greatest lies of the enemy we believe. It causes us to put our feelings into glass cases of emotion and push them as far away as we can, out of sight and out of mind. We think that if we can just pull our big-girl panties up far enough and safely tuck our emotions into the farthest corners of our hearts that we won't have to deal with the insecurity we feel and the doubt that consumes our souls. So what do we do? We go through our motherhood, treading cautiously inside our own hearts and carefully tiptoeing around these glass cases, knowing just how delicate they are.

But tiptoeing means that we can never *run free*. Tiptoeing means that we aren't living in peace. All because we choose to trust our emotions rather than the One who created us to feel them. In our tiptoeing, we're naïve enough to think that if we keep these glass cases of emotion shoved down long enough and are careful enough around them, they're never going to shatter. But when we put our emotions into those glass cases, they begin to silently multiply. And sooner or later, they're going to run out of room and shatter. And when those cases shatter, so will your precious heart. So why not be the one to choose to take the cases out, open them up, and let the Holy Spirit unpack them? We can choose, friend. We can make the choice and then let God make the change.

In your life, there is always going to be one person holding you back from the freedom of your emotions. There is always going to be one person keeping you from experiencing motherhood the way you were designed to. There is always going to be one person who doesn't believe that you have what it takes to become who you were destined to be.

And it's you. You have to be the one to take the stand and say, "No more!" to the enemy. You have to be the one who believes that what God says about you is true. And you have to be the one who looks at her emotions through the lens of Jesus and the freedom of the gospel.

It's time to take a stand to become more and be released from the bondage of our emotions. And it starts today.

Take One Step into Peace:
Surrender Your Emotions

The thing that Satan longs to steal the most from us is our identity in Christ. But Scripture tells us that Jesus came that we might have life and have it abundantly (John 10:10). God longs for us to experience life to the fullest in him, including in motherhood. But the enemy comes into our minds like a thief, and the thing he is looking to steal is our peace. And isn't that what we long for most?

Today we are going to speak peace over our emotions and declare victory over the enemy. I want you to take the emotion you feel most debilitated by today—anger, loneliness, loss of identity, insecurity, defeat, sadness—and write it on a piece of paper. Holding it in your hands, speak the prayer below to God, believing that he is capable of freeing you from this emotion that has a hold on your heart. When you are done praying, crumple your piece of paper up and be rid of it. Choose the rest of this day to continue to speak peace over your feelings, over that particular emotion, and surrender them to the Lord.

Dear God,

Today I thank you for the gift of my emotions, and that you allow me to experience your love and peace. But today my heart feels shaken. The emotions that have come along with being a mom are so hard to work through, and it's become easy to believe the lies that come along with them. But, God, I believe what you say about me and who you are! Today I give my feeling of _____ over to you. I know that you are a God of peace Who transcends all of my understanding. Please help me to guard my heart and mind against the enemy and help me to remember who I am in you. I am your child, and today I am choosing to walk in your truth for me. In Jesus' name I pray,

Amen.

Day 2

WHEN THE ENEMY TELLS YOU THAT YOU'RE NOT ENOUGH

But you are a chosen race, a royal priesthood, a holy nation, a people
for his own possession, that you may proclaim the excellencies of him
who called you out of darkness into his marvelous light.

1 PETER 2:9

I remember it like it was yesterday. It was the day that we brought our oldest daughter home from the hospital. I was a mess. Wasn't this supposed to be one of the happiest days of my life? I wanted it to be so badly, but it just wasn't. I was physically exhausted. Mentally drained. Emotionally done. Hormonally raging.

And I was so scared.

I remember sitting on our couch, and once the tears started falling, they didn't stop. As a first-time parent, I could hear the lies making their way toward the front of my mind. They were the lies of the enemy, and they shrouded me in a darkness like I had never known before.

"Your baby can't breastfeed. You are a failure."

"Your baby is losing weight. Your body is failing you."

"Will you be able to love her enough?"

"Your baby won't stop crying. You must be doing something wrong."

"You. Are. Not. Enough."

Oh, how I wish that I could go back in time and tell that new mama on the couch just how much she was worth, how much she was created to be this baby's mom. I wish I could go back and tell her that she was more than enough because God had chosen her for something great, something so much greater than herself.

She was created to be a mama empowered with the strength of Christ, proclaiming his name in the trenches of motherhood.

Now three babies later, I've seen most of it—exclusively pumping, supplementing, exclusively breastfeeding, vaginal births, a C-section, chubby babies, skinny babies, babies with colic, and a baby who doesn't make a peep...Each baby has been so different. But with each one, something remained the same.

I was enough for them, and it was because God was more than enough for me. And every time I chose to shout his name into the fear of the darkness of motherhood, the more empowered I became—even in the seasons that seemed the most hopeless. When my bones were the most dry and my voice shaky and parched, that first cry out to him in the night was always the beginning of his greatness manifested in my motherhood and his undeniable peace reigning in my life.

So, wherever you are today, mama, whether you are standing firm in your trenches or if you have fallen flat on your face, crying out for mercy from the Father...you were chosen for this. And it's not because of anything you have done, but because of the matchless grace of a God who sustains you.

No matter how dark the night may seem.

Today is your chance to take a step out of the darkness and into his marvelous light, sweet friend. God has not given you a spirit of timidity, but one of power, and of love, and of self-discipline (2 Tim. 1:7). So today is your day to declare that you belong to him and that he is great! I want you to stand up where you are right now and say these words out loud:

I am chosen by God—I am his and he is mine. I am a woman empowered by the Spirit of the Living God. The darkness of motherhood has no hold on me. Today I walk in his light!

Really, stand up and proclaim these words with your mouth and shout them in your heart. Speak them in your kitchen and your bathroom, in your baby's nursery and in your toddler's bedroom. Write them down on a card and recite them while you scrub the dishes in the sink tonight. When we proclaim the truth about who God says we are, there is a shift in the darkness. And shifting causes cracks. And one crack in the darkness may be all the space you need for that ray of hope to shine into your weary mama heart.

Dear God,

Thank you for the gift of my children. But Lord, I am fearful, weary, and insecure—the darkness of motherhood has overwhelmed me. But God, you are greater than the dark. Already, you have called me out of it and into your light and grace. Thank you for your tender mercies to me, Lord. Thank you for promising to meet me with your peace in the places of my heart that seem the most unlovable and unreachable. I praise you, for you are a God of redemption. And because you have given me the power of your Spirit, I will rise from this darkness and victoriously walk in your marvelous light. Thank you for meeting me here, Lord—thank you for being an enduring Father to this weary mama. In Jesus' name I pray,

Amen.

Day 3

WHEN YOU BRING A SACRED OFFERING

*I appeal to you therefore, brothers, by the mercies of God, to present
your bodies as a living sacrifice, holy and acceptable to God, which
is your spiritual worship. Do not be conformed to this world, but be
transformed by the renewal of your mind, that by testing you may discern
what is the will of God, what is good and acceptable and perfect.*

ROMANS 12:1–2

I've spent much of my adult years trying to keep up, especially
when it comes to being a mom. Trying to keep up with my kids,
trying to keep up with what's going on in the world, trying to
keep up with the other moms down the street, and trying to
keep up with the cooking and the cleaning and the snack making and the wiping up of spills. Most days it makes me feel
more busy than present. Have you ever found yourself feeling
this way?

This often leaves me simply going through the motions and
trying to make it until bedtime without losing my mind, only
to wake up the next morning and do it all over again. And this
busy monotony makes my purpose in the everyday with my
children seem insignificant, and my attitude toward the life I
have been given the same.

But what would happen . . .

What would happen if before my feet hit the floor in the morning, I committed myself to something more than just the mundane? If I took the moments of the day that I have been entrusted with and brought them to the place of the most holy. What if I offered up the very depths of my soul, the gift of my motherhood, as a sacred offering before the King and it became my most precious sacrifice?

If my offering of motherhood became an act of worship to God instead of just trying to keep up with the busyness of it?

I'll tell you what it would do, mama friend: *it would absolutely change everything.*

You see, when we get caught up in trying to keep up, we lose sight of the holy significance of our purpose as moms; we forget that God has chosen us for our children and that we were designed with each other in mind. Not just for our own fulfillment, but to glorify him while we carry out this calling he has given us. And this holy calling, it will always give way to joy when done with a heart of worship.

As you change diapers.

As you fold laundry.

As you discipline your children.

As you drop them off at soccer practice.

As you kiss boo-boos and stick Band-Aids on scraped knees.

As you scrub toilets.

As you rock your sweet littles in the middle of the night.

And all the while, speaking the name of Jesus to your children and extending his love and mercy to them in a way that only their mother can.

You are doing his work, Kingdom work. And it is the most

beautiful, fragrant offering you could ever lay at the feet of the Savior (Eph. 5:1–2).

I don't know about you, friend, but I don't want to scurry my way through motherhood and lose my joy in it because I'm distracted by the busyness of my tasks. I want to be a mama who holds on to these precious things that I have been given to do with hands held high and a heart surrendered to the One who created me to perform them and love my family well while doing them.

I want the busyness to fall to the wayside and my purpose of raising godly children for his glory to be renewed.

And it starts with an act of remembrance and a heart of worship.

Take One Step into Peace:
Put Up a Memorial

After the Israelites had passed through the Jordan River in Joshua 4, we read that God instructed Joshua to choose twelve men, one from each of the tribes of Israel, to pick up twelve stones to serve as a sign of remembrance, a memorial, of the goodness of God. He had delivered them into the Promised Land, and he didn't want them to forget his power and faithfulness, lest they fall into discontent. When the Israelites and their descendants would pass by these stones, they would be reminded of the promises that God kept to them, praising him for their deliverance from Egypt and the goodness that he brought them to.

As moms, it can be so easy to forget in our busyness what

God has done and what he longs to do in our lives. But today he has reminded you of the purpose in your journey of motherhood and that he is meeting you in this very moment. You did not pick up this book by mistake; God is drawing you closer to him day by day. And today we are going to make sure that you don't forget it.

Today, you are going to pick up your own stone, an object from inside of your home that reminds you of your children, and put up your own memorial to acknowledge how God is meeting you in this moment of motherhood. Put your object up in a prominent place: on your mantel or bookshelf, near your kitchen sink or in your bathroom, anywhere where you will see it daily. Let it serve as a reminder for you that each day you have is an opportunity to present God with an offering far more than just folding clothes and changing diapers, but an offering of yourself as a living sacrifice with a heart of worship.

When you start your day with this perspective and are reminded of it through the day, the way you do everything will shift to a place of peace and gratitude, and the change in your heart will be undeniable.

Dear God,

Thank you for the gift you have given me in being a mom to my children. God, I don't want to squander away the years with them by getting caught up in the busyness that so easily clouds my mind. I want to find my purpose in motherhood through you so that I can raise my children to love you and walk in your will for their lives. Help me to remember that while I am doing my everyday tasks there is purpose in them and that you delight in seeing me serve my family. Help me to remember this day that you have called me to something so much deeper than just the day-in, day-out struggles of being a mom. God, let your purpose transform my heart and redeem my motherhood, allowing me to share your love with my kids! Thank you for entrusting me with the gift of raising my children. In Jesus' name I pray,

Amen.

Day 4

WHEN YOU BELIEVE THE LIE OF LONELINESS

Nevertheless, I am continually with you;
you hold my right hand.
You guide me with your counsel,
and afterward you will receive me to glory.
Whom have I in heaven but you?
And there is nothing on earth that I desire besides you.
My flesh and my heart fail,
but God is the strength of my heart and my portion forever.

PSALM 73:23–26

We were on our way to a neighborhood barbecue, and I could feel my heart starting to race. I pulled down the mirror to double-check my hair, my growing belly bouncing with every bump we hit in the road. I reached across the console and held my husband's hand, nervously taking a deep breath. We had just moved to our new town six months prior, and I still felt like an outsider. But this barbecue was going to change everything.

Tonight, I was finally going to get out and make some new friends.

Tonight, I was going to end my streak of feeling alone.

You know how these kinds of get-togethers go, right? You

all stand around in somebody's kitchen, meet person after person, ask yourself if they like you, then ask yourself if you said something stupid, and then wonder if someone there will be your new "person." It's like speed dating, but for mom friends. These interactions had been going on for months now, and despite my best attempts, I hadn't made a solid connection with anyone. I was truly struggling to find the joy in that season of my life, and loneliness was owning my heart.

It can be hard to learn how to make new friends as a mom. Most of the time, our interactions involve going to the grocery store, having conversations at work, or scrolling through social media. And it can be more than disappointing when all we really find in those interactions are conversations that barely skim the surface, when what we really crave are intimate friendships and honest conversation outside of what we are making for dinner or what the baby's poop looks like. What we are truly desperate for is something more. For someone to look at us and really see us exactly as we are, right where we are at, and love us. For us to be able to find just one person who gets us. I think to a certain extent that we all want that as women, don't we? To find our people, love them well, and live authentically together.

To be loved and be known.

For most of us, it's what we want more than anything: real friends. But for some reason, it can be hard for us to find just one. And as time goes by while we continue to seek out these friendships but come up empty-handed, feelings of loneliness continue to chip away at our hearts, robbing us of our peace and joy. And the longer we try to hold it together, the more distressed we become.

You see, the thing about trying to contain these big emotions of loneliness is that they often turn into insecurity. And insecurity always shifts the sense of peace in a woman's heart and weakens her spirit. Loneliness whispers to me that I'm not good enough. Loneliness causes me to look at my emotions through the lens of rejection. Loneliness steals my peace and leaves me barren.

And loneliness is a lie.

In these seasons of loneliness in motherhood, the first thing that we want to do is look for friends. And while we were created for relationship, how is it that we so easily get distracted by seeking out these friendships with other women that we forget that the Most Faithful Friend longs to meet with us right now? We spend so much time waiting for God to show up that we forget that he's been right here with us all along. Sweet mama, God desires friendship with you, in seasons of plenty and in seasons of great loneliness. *But in our need to feel secure in relationships with other people, we forget that we were created with a desire to belong to him first.* And when we recognize that, it is the greatest weapon we have when the enemy tells us we are alone and aren't enough.

As the psalmist so beautifully states, we are continually with him and he is with us.

Loneliness on earth is not rejection by the Father, but rather an invitation for us to lean into him and be loved and known. You are worthy of those things. He is pursuing you today. Let's lean into him together and embrace the peace of his friendship and allow it to break the chains of our loneliness in motherhood.

As for that barbecue? Well, I walked away with an exchange of cell phone numbers and an invitation to coffee the next week. And the funny thing is, even though that coffee date never happened, that woman picked up her phone a few years later and now is one of the closest friends I have. Talk about God working all things together for my good in his perfect timing.

Take One Step into Peace:
Practice Friendship with God

So often as women we rely on interactions with other people to give us a sense of security and belonging. We text through the day, catch up with people on social media, or call a girlfriend when we are going through something hard. But today, instead of doing that, I want you to spend some time with God and in his Word. Friendship with him brings a sense of peace and belonging that no relationship this side of heaven can give you. Fighting the lie of loneliness begins with resting in the truth of the Bible and remembering who God is to us. Today I want you to find a few quiet minutes and meditate on Psalm 16. Speak it out loud. When you get to verse 5, I want you speak these words to God like you would a friend, focusing on its truth:

Oh Lord, you are my chosen portion and my cup; you hold my lot.

Friend, take joy and comfort in knowing that while you are experiencing feelings of loneliness and isolation on earth, God is more than capable of providing you with the companionship you so desperately need. You can be content in your earthly loneliness because he fills the void of the insecurity it brings. Rest in his friendship today as you speak these words of truth. Rest and let him be enough.

Dear God,

I thank you for the gift of your friendship. Not only do you love me with the heart of a Father, but you meet me in the loneliness of motherhood. I thank you that because of your friendship I am never alone. In the moments when I feel the most secluded and the most insecure, would you remind me that you are near and that you long to meet with me? Help me to put aside the constant distraction of trying to fit in and find friendship, but instead focus on my friendship with you. Thank you for loving me just as I am, Lord. And thank you for walking with me. Today I choose to find contentment and fulfillment in friendship with you. In Jesus' name I pray,

Amen.

Day 5

BUT WHAT HAPPENS WHEN YOU STILL
WANT A FRIEND?

For you formed my inward parts;
you knitted me together in my mother's womb.
I praise you, for I am fearfully and wonderfully made.

PSALM 139:13—14

And yet . . . even though God designed us for relationship with him first, he also created us with a fierce desire for friendship with others.

Did you really think that I was just going to leave you and God hanging out at a table by yourselves yesterday? No way! We were made for community, friend. God made you with a heart that longs to experience relationship and authenticity with others. And it's one of the most crucial pieces of our lives as mamas. But goodness, it can be so hard to find solid mom friends, can't it? Putting yourself out there while you're trying to find them can be even harder.

When we talked about the mom version of speed dating yesterday, I know that made so many of you cringe. Because I know that you've experienced all of the feelings of unworthiness that go along with it. I understand. I've totally felt it, too.

I constantly felt the need to hold myself back growing up. I didn't always give into that urge, but just enough so that people couldn't get the full picture of who I was. It made it hard to make real friends. It wasn't that I had a lot to hide, but it scared me to think that if people could see the truest form of myself—my biggest insecurities, my deepest emotions, and all of my personality—my soul would be met with rejection. At times, this fear of rejection would cause me to conceal parts of who God created me to be, and ultimately it denied some of the most beautiful parts of my heart to be revealed. It was in these seasons that I thought if I were to be truly vulnerable with those around me, I would become more than just seen.

That I would become fully *known*.

That fear of being known carried over into my adulthood, too—especially when trying to make friends. I would put just enough of myself out there without feeling like I was risking too much. It was a painful process, and I hated the level of guardedness I would have to put up before getting together with people—almost like I had to prepare myself not to be myself. Yet I was too insecure to take that wall down. It was absolutely exhausting, and it left me with a legit case of social anxiety.

If there is anything that I have learned in the process of making and keeping friends, it's that it doesn't matter what version of myself I put out there for the world to see; I have to be confident in who God created me to be before I can be accepted by others first. And being able to do that has come down to choosing to be vulnerable with my own heart.

Lean in close and listen up, mama: You are not a mistake. God made you and all of the beautiful parts of you on purpose. He gave you precious gifts and unique characteristics that he delights in! And I think it's just the coolest thing that he wants your friends to be able to delight in that, too. Finding your tribe—the women who will love you for your most known self—takes time. But until you choose to accept and love who God made you to be, you will never find friends because you will always be showing a false version of yourself to the world. Your future mom friends are out there waiting to find you, the truest version of who God created you to be, fearfully, wonderfully, and so uniquely made.

Take One Step into Peace:
Pray for Future Friends

When we come to the acceptance of who God made us to be, it changes how we present ourselves when we are trying to make friends. But it can still take time to find them. Many of us take the time to pray for people that we already know. But have you tried praying for people you haven't yet met who will play a significant role in your future? You are going to do that today.

Much like praying for the heart of your future spouse, it can be absolutely perspective-shifting to pray for your future friends. And seriously, how incredible will it be when that friend comes into your life and you get to tell her that you spent time praying for her? Prayer like this changes everything. It shifts our minds from worrying about what is to come and entrusting it to the One who holds it. Even your future friends.

Dear God,

I thank you for the woman you created me to be. God, would you help me to be confident in who I am? Remind me that you made me with intention and purpose, that who I am is not a mistake, and that I am worthy of finding friends just as I am. I also thank you for the gift of friendship that you designed me to experience. But right now, I am struggling to find friends. God, in all of my searching and waiting for these relationships, I trust that you will bring them to me in your timing and I pray for those women today. I ask that you would bless their lives and protect their hearts. As they walk through motherhood, remind them to be confident in who you made them to be and that you long for them to experience relationship with you and friendship with others. Be with their children and husbands, and cover their family in your protection and guidance. And, God, I already thank you for the friendships that you have in store for me. I trust in your will for my life and thank you for walking this road with me. In Jesus' name I pray,

Amen.

Day 6

WHEN YOUR EXPECTATIONS AREN'T MET

But as for me, I will watch expectantly for the LORD;
I will wait for the God of my salvation.
My God will hear me.

<small>MICAH 7:7 (NASB)</small>

The time had finally come. I had read all the books, I had watched all the YouTube videos, I had bought all the supplies, and I had been mentally preparing myself for weeks.

It was finally time for Potty Training Camp.

I was absolutely convinced that my daughter was going to be trained in three days flat. At eighteen months old (oh my gosh, what was I thinking?), she had been showing signs that she was ready for months, and I knew that we had a pee-on-the-potty prodigy. Yes, she was going to meet every expectation I had set for her, and I was going to walk away so proud. It was going to be perfect.

Except she didn't. So, neither did I. And it wasn't.

On day 3 of Potty Training Camp, I remember feeling so confused and disappointed as my daughter sat in yet another a puddle of pee on the floor. And there she sat, with tears streaming down her face, saying "Sorry" over and over again. *Why is she not getting this? Am I not doing everything right? Is there something wrong with her? Why is this not going like I thought it would? We both must be failures.*

What I didn't realize at the time was that my expectations for my daughter were completely unrealistic. In my excitement for her to reach the next milestone in her life, I had set the bar incredibly high and pressured her into doing something that she simply wasn't ready for.

We ended our last day of Potty Training Camp on a low note: she back in a diaper and me with an oversized bowl of ice cream resting on my seven-month-pregnant belly, defeated, ashamed, and so far away from perfect.

But the saddest thing? The saddest thing was that in my unrealistic expectations for her, I had set her up to fail before she even tried. How incredibly selfish of this mama.

Friend, it is imperative that we don't set unrealistic expectations for our children. Their hearts are too precious and their emotions too fragile. When we set these lofty expectations for our kids, not only does it pressure them to do something they just aren't ready for, but it puts shame in their hearts when they can't. And shame always gives way to chaos in their little souls. We have the unbelievable ability as moms to set the tone of peace in our homes, and it almost always begins with the level of expectations we establish. Are you setting the bar that is rooted in the things of the world so high that your kids are constantly trying to leap up and reach it? Or are you pointing them toward the holiness of who God wants them to be and placing his truth within their reach first?

Godliness is always the first bar that needs to be set, but it must be set in truth *and* grace.

Unrealistic expectations are almost always rooted in insecurity from a lack of perfection, especially when it comes to our motherhood. We tend to set our standards at unattainable heights, convinced that if we can just reach that next level in our lives, we will find the security we need to be confident in who we are. I don't know about you, friend, but I feel ashamed when I can't meet the expectations I set for myself, and I end up left with less security than when I started. I'm broken by the feeling of defeat when I fail, even if it's behind closed doors, especially when it comes to falling short by God's standards. And this feeling of shame, this agony of defeat, it's crushing my soul. And in my selfishness, I'm taking my kids' souls right along with mine when I project these expectations of perfection on them. It sets all of us up to fail. None of us stands a chance.

But when our expectations are rooted in Christ and we remember that he has already chosen us, we can *expect* him to give us the security we need, because he already took care of it on the cross. It sets us on a journey over the course of a lifetime of transformation and growth. And while a lifetime may seem long, doesn't it take the pressure off of you to set the expectation of doing everything perfect *right now*? And aren't you so tired of trying so hard to do it all just right, friend? I'm tired, but I'm also ready for more of Jesus and learning to wait expectantly on him while he changes me.

Take One Step into Peace:
Laying Down Our Expectations

When we sit down and examine our hearts, we can see that the list of unrealistic expectations we have set for ourselves and our children is overwhelming. We break our hearts trying to do more than we are capable of simply because we think it will bring us the peace we desire. But today we are going to let one of those things go. By practicing momentary release of things that consume our lives, we are able to discern whether or not they are things that we need to lower our expectations of or be rid of permanently.

There was a season in my life that I felt like I needed to be perfectly put together every single day: makeup, clothes, hair, everything. It took away from my time with God in the mornings and was causing me to obsess over my image. But by practicing momentary release of some of those things, I was able to see how much beauty had a hold on my heart. And the peace I began to experience when I let go of that unrealistic expectation was so freeing.

So, what expectation is ruling in your heart today, mama? Maybe you struggle with keeping the house perfect or being involved in every single activity at your kids' school. Maybe you have the expectation that your baby is supposed to breastfeed, and after months of struggling, she still just can't get it, and it's stealing joy from your motherhood. Or maybe you're setting so many expectations outside of godliness that it's drawing you further away from him and closer to the false perfection of the world.

Lay your unrealistic expectations at the foot of the cross today. There's no better place to leave them, and no better place to receive his peace.

Dear God,

Today, I've realized that I have set up so many unrealistic expectations for me and for my children. But God, today is also the day that I am going to take a step forward in letting those expectations go. I pray that you would take these things that I feel like I have to do and release me from the hold they have on my heart. Help me to recognize that growing in you is something that I will continue to have to work at, and that your purification is the only thing that will give me the peace I need. God, I also ask you to equip me with grace for my children. Help me to hold them up against your standards, not against the selfish ones I think they should meet. I lay these expectations at your feet today, God, trusting that while I wait for you to grow my character, you will also soften my heart. In Jesus' name I pray,

Amen.

Day 7

WHEN OUR SEX LIFE MEETS OUR PRAYER LIFE

This is the confidence we have in approaching God: that if we ask anything according to his will, he hears us.

1 JOHN 5:14 (NIV)

A few months after my husband and I had our second child, we were still trying to get back into the groove of things. Sex wasn't physically uncomfortable anymore, but I was emotionally drained and discouraged. I had the expectation that things in the bedroom would bounce back just as easily as it had with our first. Was I ever wrong. We both longed to have some time together, so in a desperate attempt to be intimate while our oldest was napping, we tried to put our colicky baby down for a nap (and by colicky, I mean that girl cried 24/7 except when she was eating).

As my husband got her settled in the crib, I hurried into the bathroom to try and get myself somewhat presentable. I ran a brush through my hair, put on some mascara, and brushed my teeth. As I looked up from the sink, I stared into the mirror. *I can't believe he would want any of this*, I said to myself. I sat down on the toilet seat and looked down at my naked body: my postpartum tummy was jiggly and moved in ways I thought only Jell-O could, my boobs were leaking milk everywhere because I could hear the baby crying, my face was tired, and no amount of makeup could ever cover the adult acne I had going on. In a mad dash, I walked into our room, threw on a bra, promptly turned off the lights, pulled the covers up over my body and waited for my husband to come in.

I had a big problem and I was terrified to tell him: *I didn't want him to look at me while I was naked.*

This routine went on for a couple of months, and finally I just couldn't take it any longer. After weeks of him asking me if something was wrong, it all came out. I told him that I didn't want him to see my body. As five postpartum chins emerged below my face, I blubbered and sobbed as I told him where my insecure heart was and how I just wanted to feel like myself again, how I wanted to feel like *us*. That I wanted sex to be normal and that I would feel beautiful.

And do you know what that man did? He prayed over me. He held me close and prayed that I would know and feel my beauty. He prayed that we would enjoy sex. He prayed that I would be confident again. Over the sobs of his jiggly wife and the cries of his colicky infant, his prayers over me gave me a starting point to allow God into our sex life and restore the pieces of my insecure heart.

It changed everything.

You see, when we are fighting in this war for intimacy in our marriages, we aren't bringing the biggest piece of weaponry to the table: we aren't praying about our sex lives. Whether you are insecure like I was, find yourself too tired to be intimate, are in a dry spell in your sex life, are experiencing physical pain, or just have a hard heart toward your husband, prayer changes everything. *Including sex.*

Adding prayer into the equation of our sex lives is one of the most important things we can do as wives. It must be a priority for us weary mamas. You can start moving toward sexual healing today. Put down your phone, remove any distractions, walk into your bedroom, and sit on your bed and pray. Pray that you could be confident in who God made you to be on this very day. Pray that you can be vulnerable with your spouse. Pray for energy. Pray for sex to be a priority. Believe that God can help you experience growth and intimacy in your marriage. Pray that if there is physical pain, it would cease. Thank him for the gift of sex. And, ladies, boldly come before God and pray for awesome sex with your husband, then be confident that God can bless this part of your marriage. God created physical intimacy to be a good thing. And because of that, I think he cares enough to listen to our prayers about what's going on in the bedroom.

Philippians 4:6 says, "Do not be anxious about anything, but in *every situation*, by prayer and petition, with thanksgiving, present your requests to God" (NIV; emphasis added).

Yes, every situation. Even sex.

Dear God,

Thank you for the gift of sex in our marriage. Thank you for creating it to be beautiful and fulfilling. But Lord, right now we are struggling in our sex lives. God, I am inviting you to come in and restore it. I pray for a renewed sense of intimacy with my husband; help us to be vulnerable with one another and honest in our conversations. I pray that you would go before us in the bedroom, Lord. Help us to make sex a priority and give us the energy to make it happen. Being a mama can be exhausting, but God I want to be able to give the best of me to my husband. I pray a blessing on our sex life and invite you in to restore and renew this part of our marriage. And Lord, I pray for our sex to be amazing and fulfilling—because that's what you created it to be. In Jesus' name I pray,

Amen.

Day 8

WHEN MAMA GETS ANGRY

A soft answer turns away wrath,
but a harsh word stirs up anger.

PROVERBS 15:1

"Seriously, just be quiet for five freaking minutes!"

The words spewed out of my mouth before I could stop them. They came from the deepest part of my tired mama soul, and once they started they just kept coming. It wasn't so much the words, but how I said them, how I screamed them at my daughter.

I will never forget the look in her eyes that day. The moment I saw her face was the moment I knew I was wrong. My oldest backed away from me as I yelled at her; she was afraid of her mommy. In an instant, I knew I had a problem; it had just been getting worse over the last few months—I had uncontrolled mom anger. Something had to change, and it had to change fast. Because being angry is one of the most shameful places to be.

That night I lay in bed next to my sweet sleeping girl and promised to do better for her. Not only did I promise that my actions would change, but that I would get to the root of the problem: I didn't need a quick fix, I knew that my heart would need a transformation. After looking back over the last few months, I realized that my temper had become incredibly short with my girls and that I was yelling more than I ever had before. And the heart of harshness that came out in my actions and my words was affecting everyone around me, especially them. As mamas, we have such a huge responsibility to set the tone for our homes and our children's souls. It's perhaps one of the most important roles we have.

But how do we get to the root of the problem?

We've got to learn to *slow down*.

Know this, my beloved brothers: let every person be quick to hear, slow to speak, slow to anger; for the anger of man does not produce the righteousness of God. JAMES 1:19–20

Have you ever noticed that when mom anger boils up in us that it's usually when we're in a hurry? Take a look back at your last twenty-four hours, and you will see that when you were angry with your kids you were probably rushing around: rushing to get out the door, rushing to get household chores done, or rushing your kids to get the words out of their mouths without it taking them all day. But when we make a conscious choice with our kids to stop, step back, and listen, our reactions toward our kids change drastically. And when our reactions toward our kids change, the angry mom beast inside slowly becomes tame. When our mom anger becomes tame, our hearts *change*. And ladies, our kids notice when there is a change that's that big in their mamas. Because it's a change that's so much more than just something we come up with on our own. It's something bigger.

It's the transformation by the Holy Spirit. And it has to start with slowing down and turning our harsh words into gentle ones.

Today I want you to think of the one situation with your kids that makes you the angriest, and I want you to do it. Whether it's preparing a meal, bath-time routine, folding laundry, working on homework, you need to put yourself in that situation. But before you start, I want you to intentionally *pause* before you begin. Take a few moments to think about the situation you are about to go into and recognize that it is probably going to be hard. Next ask the Lord to quiet your heart before you begin your task and pray for patience and for his Spirit to go before you and your children. Just those few minutes to take a breather before your anger trigger will make all the difference in the world—for how you react and how your kids see your heart changing. One slow-down moment at a time.

Dear God,

I have found myself getting so angry with my kids lately and I am so ashamed. But God, you can remove the anger in my heart and remove my shame. I need your help to take the time to slow down with my children, Lord. Please help me in situations that make me angry and fill me with your peace and patience as I parent my children. God, I don't want to be an angry mom, but I know that I cannot do it alone. Please help me to be gentle and merciful with my children, as you are always gentle and merciful with me. Thank you so much for loving me and forgiving me for the anger I have in my heart. In Jesus' name I pray,

Amen.

Day 9

WHEN YOU'RE ASKED TO MAKE
ANOTHER DOZEN COOKIES

Someone may say, "I'm allowed to do anything," but not everything is helpful. I'm allowed to do anything, but not everything encourages growth.

1 CORINTHIANS 10:23 (GW)

My phone buzzed on the kitchen counter, and I reluctantly picked it up. I knew exactly what was about to go down.

"Hey, mama! We have this picnic coming up next week at the park. Do you think you could bring a dozen cookies? Maybe two dozen? I know you're already bringing a salad, but some cookies would really help."

I could hear the desperation in her voice on the other end of the line. If only she could hear it in my mind.

"Um, yeah. Sure, I can bring a couple dozen," I said reluctantly, trying to convince myself that I could actually make two dozen cookies, a salad, *and* get myself to the picnic with my two kids while trying to not lose my own cookies during month 2 of my third pregnancy.

What on earth are you thinking? How are you going to be able to do all of that? You can't add another thing to your list this week, I thought. And despite hearing that little voice in the back of my mind telling me to say no, I still felt like I needed to say yes to that question on the phone call. I still felt like I couldn't turn her down. I still felt like I needed to bring the cookies.

I still felt like I needed to please.

I don't know about you, friend, but I ride the struggle bus when it comes to learning how to say no. I feel like if I don't agree to what is asked of me that I will let that person down or they will think that I'm selfish. This sudden rush of needing to please fills my chest, my mind starts to race, and before I know it the words "Yes, of course!" come fumbling out of my mouth, and once again I've committed to something I know I should have said no to. And ultimately, I care more about what they think rather than the health of my own heart and the sanity of my mind.

All because I want to say yes to something that doesn't really matter in the long run.

Well, I've got news for you, mama friend. A dozen cookies doesn't matter in light of eternity. But I'll tell you something that does. Your time. Your time is precious to God. And how you choose to spend it matters to him even more. Paul talks about this in I Corinthians. He says that there are a lot of things that we can do in this life, but not all of them are in our best interest. There are a lot of options of how we can spend our time, but we don't have to choose every single one.

We always have the opportunity to say yes, but we are allowed to say no.

As moms, there are a lot of things that this world is going to try to tell us we have to do. We feel pressured to buy the latest stroller, we get bombarded by what types of baby food are the safest, the mom down the street scrutinizes how we discipline our kids, we rack our brains over what kind of preschool to send our little ones to, and we feel pressured that we have to be involved in every single activity our kids are offered . . . or that we always need to bring a dozen cookies to the picnic.

You have the choice to say no to the cookies. You have the power to say no to all of it. If it's something that isn't going to bring you joy or give God glory without losing your ever-loving mind, I am giving you permission to say no today so that you can say yes to something greater tomorrow.

Take One Step into Peace:
Make Your Lists

I don't know about you, but making lists is therapeutic for me. Not only that, but it gives me a realistic sense of my time and where my heart is. Today I want you to find a few quiet minutes and write out your list for today, this week, and the next month. What events do you have coming up? What did you sign up for? Does your schedule leave room for flexibility? Is there time available to be together just as a family? Is there space for you to take a couple hours to breathe? Where does spending time investing in your relationship with God fall into place, or did it even make the list? I want you to really look at these lists. Pray over what is on those lists. Decide what needs to stay and what needs to go. If you can't cross anything off your list, reevaluate if you should have said yes to it in the first place. While you may have said yes to something once doesn't mean you have to make that same choice again. You can learn to say no. You can learn to discern. God loves to give us wisdom when we ask him for it. Ephesians 5:15–16 says, "Look carefully then how you walk, not as unwise but as wise, making the best use of the time, because the days are evil." We can be wise with our time and our choices. Wisdom starts in looking through the lens of eternity.

Dear God,

I thank you for the gifts of choice and time. But in a world with so many choices and so little time, I can feel so overwhelmed in knowing how to make the right decisions for me and my family. God, would you grant me wisdom to know how I make my decisions? Give me discernment in when to say yes and when to say no. Lord, I pray that you would give me the confidence to prioritize my time well, making the most of it, knowing that my time is precious. Thank you for giving me wisdom in making choices that honor and glorify you. In Jesus' name I pray,

Amen.

Day 10

WHEN MAMA NEEDS WISDOM

*If any of you lacks wisdom, let him ask God, who gives generously to all
without reproach, and it will be given to him. But let him ask in faith,
with no doubting, for the one who doubts is like a wave of the sea that is
driven and tossed by the wind.*

JAMES 1:5–6

I remember standing in the baby aisle at Target with my bar
code scanner, looking at all of the diapers in tears. I had read
all of the reviews online and asked every other mama I knew,
and it was finally time to make my choice. It was down to Hug-
gies and Pampers, and I was pretty sure that the stress of this
decision was going to send me into early labor. It wasn't the lack
of confidence I had in either of the two brands that made this
such an emotional moment for me; rather, it was the lack of
confidence I had in myself to make the right choice.

Because this was *my baby*, and gosh darn it, I was going to make
the right decision for her and her bottom. The only problem
was, I had no idea what I was doing. And there was no way I was
going to let anyone else know it, either.

I didn't know it at the time, but that day in the diaper aisle
was a defining moment for me. It was the first of many choices
that I had to make for my daughter that would send my heart

over the edge and my mind into the constant guessing game of *Am I doing the right thing?* A few months later, I would find myself back in that same Target, just one aisle over. The decision of what brand of sweet potatoes to let my daughter try first just about brought me to my knees. And there I was once again, trapped in doubt and believing the lie that the wisdom of my choice wasn't good enough.

The thing is, friend, big decision or not, the weight of wanting to choose well for our children can be crippling if we allow it to be, often leaving us with a sense of regret after we've made a choice. But trusting in the God who freely hands out wisdom to his children when they ask for it is not only empowering, but it ushers in a sense of peace when the insecurity of our minds starts to take over.

I hate to be the one to tell you this, but there are going to be a lot bigger, a lot harder decisions in motherhood coming your way. Decisions that shape the souls of your children and alter the course of your family in ways that you never dreamed you would be responsible for. This isn't just about comparing labels, contrasting brands, and reading every how-to baby book we can get our hands on—that's just gaining knowledge from people who think they have it all figured out. But *wisdom*—now we're talking guidance of the heart that is rooted in the truth of God's character.

You have been given the responsibility of choosing well for your children. You have been entrusted with this precious gift in helping to shape their souls and point them toward eternity.

When you seek the wisdom of God through prayer and the Bible, your life is suddenly turned from the chaos of choices to the confidence of his peace. No longer are you tossed to and fro in the indecisiveness of your minds, but you become a woman who is confident in the choices she makes for herself and her family because of the God who sustains her to make them.

Mama, I can guarantee you that you aren't going to stand before God at the end of your life and have him say, "You should have chosen the organic sweet potatoes." No, friend! He is going to say, "You chose me and my character when you needed to make a decision. You asked me for wisdom; I gave it to you, and you were obedient to walk in it. Well done, good and faithful mama!" Let's not allow the chaos of choice to consume our motherhood, friend. Let's let the peace of his wisdom lead us, instead.

Take One Step into Peace:
Ask for Wisdom

As a mom, you have so many decisions you have to make for your children on any given day. But have you prayed for wisdom in how to make those decisions? So often, we find ourselves scouring the internet for the advice of the "experts" but forget to take it to the Lord in prayer before we begin. When we begin our choices in God's peace, it always gives way to clarity of mind, allowing us to make a wise decision. So ask boldly for his wisdom today.

Dear God,

I thank you that you are a God who is full of wisdom and longs to give it to me. Today I have realized that I have not been coming to you for it in prayer or seeking it in your Word. But I want to change that today, Lord. Would you grant me wisdom with _____. As I am making this decision, I ask that you would give my mind clarity and that I would not get overwhelmed with the choices I have been given. God, you gave me a mind that is able to make good choices, and I trust that you are going to help guide me in making those. Thank you for your wisdom and thank you for your peace. In Jesus' name I pray,

Amen.

Day 11

WHEN ANGER BECOMES RESENTMENT

"In your anger do not sin." Do not let the sun go down while you are still angry, and do not give the devil a foothold.

Ephesians 4:26–27 (niv)

I heard the back door close and my husband's footsteps coming down the hallway. My heart grew a little angrier with each step he took. He was home almost two hours later than when he said he would be, and he hadn't even bothered to text me, telling me he would be delayed.

He walked into the kitchen, the kids clamoring around him, squealing with delight. I didn't even turn around from my sink full of dishes. "Hey, Babe, sorry I'm late. I must have lost track of time."

"It's fine," I mumbled as I kept scrubbing the grease from my skillet, trying not to whip around and blow up at him. *If he only knew the day I had here at home. If he only knew how much I needed him to be home when he said he was going to be. Does he even care that I'm struggling? If he only understood,* I thought. My anger was growing by the minute, and I decided that I was going to give him the silent treatment and just get on with our evening.

But before I turned around to walk out of the room, I felt a gentle tug break through my feisty spirit:

I know you're mad. I know you're hurt. But you cannot stay angry, Lauren. I love your husband just like I love you. Do not let the enemy win. Do not walk away in your anger.

I turned around and looked at my husband, the man I loved but at the moment didn't like very much. And in that moment, I made a choice—I chose a moment of grace over an evening of anger. I shuffled over to him and gave him a hug, "I'm glad you're home. I had a really hard day; can we talk about it?"

So, there we stood in the kitchen and talk we did. I told him about the stress of my day, about how his being late and not calling stressed me out even more. And I told him about how angry I was and how he had made me feel. He apologized, and we talked through ways that we could communicate better. He told me how hard his day had been, too. We embraced one another in a new understanding. And then I did something that softened my heart toward my husband and the Father even more: I apologized to my husband for planning against him in anger.

I told him I was sorry for thinking about an evening rooted in resentment and hard feelings. I apologized for letting my heart harden before we even spoke.

I realized how ten minutes of conversation with an authentic desire to understand each other changed everything for us that night. Instead of going to bed angry, we went to bed in peace that was found in forgiveness.

Five years ago, that moment in the kitchen never would have happened. Five years ago, I would have chosen to continue the evening in my anger, remain quiet, and silently hang his faults over his head. Five years ago, I would have let the sun go down on my anger and, in the morning, woken up in resentment. But by understanding the grace of God and his plan for redemption in our marriage, my heart had been softened, and the enemy's foothold taken out from under him.

You see, friend, the thing about Satan is that he knows our weaknesses. He studies our habits and he knows the parts of our hearts that are most susceptible to sin. And for many of us, holding anger against our husbands is a place that the enemy sinks his teeth into the easiest because anger is one of the most blinding emotions we have. And while feeling anger isn't a sin, staying in it is.

Anger is the number one thing that Satan wants us to hang on to in our marriages. But not today, Satan. Today this mama is walking in God's peace and not giving you any room in her marriage.

Take One Step into Peace:
Letting Go of Anger

As women, we tend to remember most of the faults committed against us, don't we? We hang on to painful words or shut down when our feelings have been hurt, especially in our marriages. Today is the day that you are going to start digging through some of these burdens of anger that are buried deep within your heart. I want you to look back at the last week with your spouse and search your heart—was there something that happened that caused you to be mad at him? If there was something, it probably won't take you very long to remember it, because you will have a strong feeling associated with it. Once you have this instance in your mind, think about the way you reacted to the situation. Did you talk to him about it and explain your feelings? Did you shout at him in anger or did you sweep it under the rug?

For a lot of us, we often hold these feelings of anger back and let our hearts become resentful; we pull up the big-girl panties and put our emotions into the glass cases. But today I want you to sit down with your husband and tell him how this particular instance made you feel—not bashing him for what he did, but simply explaining how his actions affected your heart and your attitude toward him. Then, I want you to ask for his forgiveness. I know this is a hard one. But admitting your own sin in the situation not only softens your heart toward the Father, but it also softens your heart toward your husband, and his toward you.

Dear God,

   I thank you for the gift of my marriage and the joy that it brings me. But recently I have also been experiencing anger in my marriage and secretly holding on to bitterness against my husband. I know that hanging on to this anger is a sin and unhealthy for my marriage. God, I long to have these chains broken so that I can have a marriage that is full of forgiveness and your love. But I can't do that if I don't come to you with my sin first. Please forgive me for the anger that I have been hanging on to toward my husband. I ask, Lord, that you take away these feelings that don't honor you and allow my husband and me to have the conversations we need to have in order to move forward. Being open about this is so scary, but God, I trust that you will give me the courage to talk to my husband about these feelings. Thank you for loving me, thank you for loving my husband, and thank you for being a Father who forgives. In Jesus' name I pray,

Amen.

Day 12

WHEN YOUR MOM BOD BECOMES YOUR IDOL

Or do you not know that your body is a temple of the Holy Spirit within you, whom you have from God? You are not your own.

1 CORINTHIANS 6:19

I remember desperately trying to squeeze into my favorite pair of jeans about six months after having my son. They were a lot tighter than I thought they would be, as I pulled them up over my thighs and cinched them shut around my waist.

This is just ridiculous; I should be able to fit into these by now, I told myself. I was embarrassed that they didn't fit. From that moment on I vowed that I was going to lose the last of my baby weight. There was absolutely nothing that was going to stop me from fitting back into those jeans.

For a solid month, I gave it everything I had. I counted my calories, worked out every single day, drank nothing but water, and stood in front of the mirror each morning, scrutinizing every roll and lump in my post-baby body. I did everything I possibly could; even my last waking thoughts were consumed by how I could lose the weight faster. But at the end of that month, I still hadn't lost any more weight. And I still didn't fit into those jeans.

All I was left with was an insecure heart and a pair of pants that were still too small, crumpled up in the corner of my closet.

After a few days of sulking and eating a sleeve of Oreos that I had hidden in my closet, I decided that I needed to take some extra time in prayer. I had been so consumed over the last month with trying to lose my baby weight that I was feeling pretty disconnected from the Lord. So on the floor of my closet, with the pair of still-too-small pants lying in the corner, I sat with my Bible and a few of my Oreos and did my best to let the Lord speak to my insecure heart.

I opened my Bible to the Psalms and came up on chapter 34:4–5, "I sought the LORD, and he answered me; he delivered me from all my fears. Those who look to him are radiant; their faces are never covered with shame" (NIV).

I paused and read those words over and over again. And after each time reading them, I looked over at the crumpled pair of jeans. For the thirty days, I hadn't been seeking the Lord at all—I had been seeking the perfection of the world instead of purification by my Father's heart. I glanced over at the mirror and stared into my tired face. There was no look of radiance; there was only shame—no, not because I still couldn't fit into the jeans, but because I had wasted an entire month replacing my time with the Lord with time obsessing over an old pair of pants.

As mamas in our culture today, it can be so hard to find the balance of being confident in our bodies and what they are capable of and not being consumed by their size. We scrutinize the number on the tag of our pants rather than the content of our hearts. And more often than not, we give our attention to the outside of our bodies but neglect the matters of the soul—the parts that God cares about so much more than the size pants we wear. What we must continue to ask ourselves is this: Are our bodies our temple or our idol?

For me, the day that I realized that my jeans still didn't fit, I saw that my body had become an idol. And it needed to be knocked down off of the throne that it held in my heart.

Take One Step into Peace:
Knock Down Idols

I want you to go into your closet and try on a few pairs of your pants. Don't look at the number on the tag, but put them on and see how you feel in them. Once you've found the most comfortable pair, I want you to get down on the floor and play with your kids. Now this is important, so I want you to really hone in on this: I want you to remember how you feel when you are playing on the floor while you are wearing those pants. Do you feel joy while you roll around and play? Do you feel comfortable while you lie on the couch and read a book? Do you feel loved when your babies wrap their arms around your waist and tell you they love you? Remember those feelings. And remember that the number on the tag of your jeans does not determine the joy you get from being with your children. And it definitely does not determine the joy you get from spending time with God. Choose a healthy temple, but don't let it be your idol any longer.

Dear God,

I thank you for my body. Thank you for the gift of being able to carry my child. But as my body continues to shift and change, I pray that you would first give me confidence in you and that you would continue to remind me to look to you first and not to the yearnings of this world. I pray that you would help me to keep my body healthy so that I can be a strong and active mom. But more so I pray that you would give me the power to seek your wisdom first so that I may be a mother who is confident in your love for me and grounded in your truth. Thank you for loving me, Lord. In Jesus' name I pray,

Amen.

Day 13

WHEN COMPARISON STICKS ITS FOOT IN THE DOOR

For though we walk in the flesh, we are not waging war according to the flesh. For the weapons of our warfare are not of the flesh but have divine power to destroy strongholds. We destroy arguments and every lofty opinion raised against the knowledge of God, and take every thought captive to obey Christ.

2 CORINTHIANS 10:3–5

I have struggled with comparison my entire life. If I look back on any trial I've gone through, any season that has been painful, the cause of each of those situations was almost always rooted in comparison.

For some reason, I actually thought that motherhood was going to change all of that. I naïvely assumed that I would feel a deeper sense of security and fulfillment once I finally had a baby in my arms. If only I knew that motherhood would be one of the places that comparison would affect my heart the most—once again leaving me disappointed and searching for security and peace in the places I had no business looking for it.

Most would say that comparison is the thief of joy, but theft seems too instantaneous for me. Yes, comparison steals my joy, but it's more like an animal gnawing away on a carcass. It's slow and drawn out, repetitive and ugly. It doesn't just take my joy all at once, but it takes it away little by little. It's a war waged against something far more precious than just my flesh—it's a war that's fighting for my soul, telling me that I need more of what the world has to offer and less of the holiness of Christ. It's a war that is won one little glance at a time.

So how do we battle this ugliness that continues to come around in our hearts again and again?

We keep our eyes set on Jesus, friend. And it starts by making sure our first thought is to look only to him.

I think that as moms, it's so easy for us to have drifting eyes, you know? It's like we have FOMO (fear of missing out). When my eyes see something flashy, they suddenly become focused on it and nothing else. I see a friend on Facebook in a bathing suit who looks better in hers than I do in mine, I walk through my neighbor's front door and her house is spotless, or I can even go so far as to look at another couple's marriage and wish that mine seemed as perfect. That's when I tend to get worried about what the rest of the world is doing and what they've got that I don't. After one little glance, I grow consumed by what I'm missing out on and start to obsess over how I can get it, becoming fixated on how I think it will make me feel once it's mine. And all of that takes my eyes where? Off of Jesus.

That's when my focus shifts, my eyes start to drift, and comparison sticks its foot in the door. That is usually when insecurity starts to take a foothold in my heart. And Satan loves the weakness of comparison in my heart, friend. Because he knows that I have the tendency to think that I can achieve what I want by myself and find security in what *I* can do and who *I* have become on my own. But when I look to Jesus and realize what he has done for me compared to what I deserve? That's when I fight comparison the hardest. It makes Satan shudder to know with whom I can fight my insecurity the most: *Christ and his work on the cross.*

Dear friend, there is no greater security than knowing that the God of the universe sent his Son to pay the penalty for your sins on the cross. You don't need to take part in comparison because you are already loved enough that Jesus would die for you! Talk about security-inducing.

When we declare Jesus as our security, things change. When we proclaim his greatness over the mere wants and desires of this world that we so often long for, our perspective shifts and his peace reigns in our hearts. And when we begin to take every thought captive, taking our eyes off of the world and looking at Jesus, everything changes.

Where there was once insecurity, now there is assurance.

Where there was bondage, now there is freedom.

Where there was rubble, now there is a cornerstone.

Where there was chaos, now there is peace.

Where there was doubt, now there is trust.

Where there was darkness, now there is hope.

Where there was frustration, now there is encouragement.

And where there was once comparison, now there is confidence in Christ. No longer am I constantly obsessing over the things that once consumed my mind. Instead I'm filled with the satisfaction of his love for me. I become content without the need to compare. I am satisfied in him, and him alone.

Do you see the pattern here? In order to find our true confidence and be rid of comparison, we have to come to grips with everything we aren't so we can stand in awe of everything that he is. Lifting the curtain of comparison doesn't start with us keeping our eyes on ourselves; it begins and finishes with us keeping our eyes on Jesus. As we continue to take each thought captive and stand in the worthiness of Christ, the rest of the world is going to fade away; our tendency to slip back into comparison will be gone because the love of Jesus is just that much better. He's better than the mom next door, he's better than the celebrity on TV, and he's certainly better than the mom the world tells us we need to be. Because of the victory that we have in the cross, we can stand confident and secure in God's love for us.

Comparison has no place in the heart of a woman who is chosen and loved by God.

Take One Step into Peace:
Breaking the Bondage of Comparison

I want you to think about the one thing that you compare yourself with the most, and today you are going to declare victory over it in your heart. It shouldn't be hard to figure out what it is; you immediately thought of it when you read the word *comparison* in the title of today's devotional. I want you to take that one thing and speak it gone to the enemy.

Satan, I will not let you have a foothold in my heart. I am a daughter of the King, and he has redeemed me! No longer will I let the comparison of _____ reign in my heart, but instead I cry out for and take hold of the peace of Christ, which comes through the cross. I am confident in Jesus, not my insecurity. You don't have room to be here any longer, Satan.

In the name of Jesus, I command you to leave and take my insecurity of comparison with you!

Friend, there is power in speaking the name of Jesus to the enemy! Say these words with confidence; speak them when the first thought of comparison begins to sneak into your mind. Take your thoughts captive and fight the war that is raging in your precious soul.

Dear God,

I thank you for sending your Son to die on the cross for my sins when I didn't deserve it. There is no greater sense of security in this world than the security of your love for me. Today I take that love and put it in the place where comparison reigns in my heart. God, I ask that whenever I begin to feel comparative thoughts or feelings, you would quickly replace them with the truth of your love for me and who you call me as your child. May I be reminded that you love me as I am and that it is your peace that I should be seeking instead of what the world has to offer. Thank you for the gift of my security in you. In Jesus' name I pray,

Amen.

Day 14

WHEN MAMA GETS HER JOY BACK

May the God of hope fill you with all joy and peace in believing, so that by the power of the Holy Spirit you may abound in hope.

ROMANS 15:13

I think one of the things that surprised me the most about becoming a mom was how much I didn't feel like myself.

It sounds silly, right? If being a mom was now a part of my identity, then why did I feel more unlike myself than ever before? I found that being a mom consumed so much of who I was in certain seasons of parenthood, especially in the first year of each of my children's lives. It wasn't that I didn't love being a mom; it was just that I didn't seem to have the time or energy to be anyone else. And with each subsequent child I had, I lost a little more of who I was, buried beneath the diapers, laundry, toys, and school drop-off lines. Over time, the person I knew I was and the things that brought me joy seemed to slip further and further away.

After having our third child, I was diagnosed with post-partum depression. It was during this particular season that I felt unlike myself in an entirely new way. No matter what I did or how high I tried to pull up my big-girl panties, everything about me felt inauthentic and lost. It was one of the loneliest times of my entire life. And remember what loneliness does? It steals your peace and leaves you barren.

And wow, was I ever barren.

One of the best pieces of advice I received after being diagnosed with postpartum depression came from my pastor's wife. She had also walked the road of depression and the feeling of being lost associated with it. She and her husband were some of the first people I spoke with after realizing that something was very wrong with my mind and my heart.

As I sat hunched over in their living room chair crying in shame at my darkness, one thing she suggested to try stuck out to me. She told me to pick one small thing that my old self would love and choose to do it every single day. She told me I had to be intentional about making it happen, even if I didn't feel like it, and that slowly my mind would catch up with what I knew I loved in my heart. "I promise you, Lauren, you're in there. God is going to bring you joy again. And sometimes that joy comes in something familiar."

So that's what I did. I went home that day and I made my choice. My depression was so deep at this point that it took everything in me to do it, but I did my very favorite thing: I lit my fall-scented candle. The aroma filled my kitchen that afternoon as I scrubbed a sink full of dishes, and I felt nothing. *This is ridiculous*, I thought. *How is lighting this candle going to help me find my joy again? How is God going to use this to heal me?* But I continued to follow her instruction.

Day after day, like clockwork, I woke up and lit that candle. And slowly, ever so slowly, a little bit of the darkness started to turn into light in my kitchen. Not all of it, but a little. And as the light of my candle continued to flicker, so did the spark of hope in my soul. But only because I continued to *choose well*.

It wasn't just lighting that candle that brought me hope. One of the other things that I chose to do during this season was to continue to go back to what God's Word said about trusting him. When I would light my candle, I would look up to the verses taped onto my kitchen cabinet, and I would pray one specific verse each morning out loud to the God who saw me in my wandering:

May the God of hope fill you with all joy and peace in believing, so that by the power of the Holy Spirit you may abound in hope.   ROM. 15:13

There was so much power in speaking words of truth to my own heart, friend. And there is that same power at your fingertips, too. By meditating on this truth and trusting that God would meet me in my darkness, the Holy Spirit continued to show up day after day and filled my life with hope again. And as hope rose inside of me, the joy and peace of Jesus followed suit.

But it never would have happened if I wasn't diligent in choosing to do that one thing that was familiar to my heart and meditating on God's Word each morning. I truly believe that when we begin our day in God's promises for us, it has the ability to drastically crush the enemy's lies underneath our feet and recenter our emotions. Satan loves for us to feel rushed first thing in the morning and forget whose we are and what our purpose is. But when we speak these truths into our own lives, we are reminded that God is worthy of our trust and that he will be faithful to bring us into his peace once again.

My pastor's wife was right; I was still in there. And so was my joy.

He did it for me, and I know he can do it for you, too, mama friend.

I know that who you are might seem buried beneath the weight of motherhood today. I know that it seems like there just isn't enough time in the day to find yourself or practice self-care. While self-care alone will never satisfy the need for God, it is still so important! God created you to love and enjoy certain things, and he longs for you to do so. I want you to choose one thing and continue to do it every morning for the rest of the month. For me, it was lighting a candle. Perhaps you like to take a walk by yourself, read a book, spend some time alone drinking your coffee, open the windows, or turn on your favorite music. But before you do these things, I want you to take a few moments to recite the Scripture above out loud. Speak it to God in the prayer below and trust that in the midst of the messiness of motherhood you can take intentional time to find joy. He will deliver it to you.

Dear God,

Thank you for giving me the gift of motherhood. But today I feel lost in it. I feel as if I can't find myself or take the time to do something that I enjoy. God, I know that you long to meet me in these moments and fill my heart with joy. Allow me to find some time in my day to meditate on your Word and do something that brings me peace. I know that you can fill me with these things because my hope is in your promises for me. Would your Holy Spirit meet me today and remind me of who I am in you? Thank you for loving me and knowing me, God, even when I have lost sight of myself. In Jesus' name I pray,

Amen.

Day 15

WHEN MOM FEAR IS CONSUMING

I have said these things to you, that in me you may have peace. In the world you will have tribulation. But take heart; I have overcome the world.

JOHN 16:33

Fear.

It's a word that causes us to crumble from the inside out as mothers. Fear is universal, yet it looks different for each one of us, doesn't it? The thing about fear is that giving in to it during one moment of weakness can send our entire day spiraling out of control and gives peace a swift kick out the door. Especially when it comes to our children.

When my oldest was about a month old, a local girl was abducted while walking to school. For days, I bounced my little baby and was glued to the news, praying with this young girl's family that she would be found safe. At the end of their five-day search they found that precious little girl brutally murdered. And for the first time, I sat in our house while I held my baby girl and wept for the loss of someone else's, dreading what would happen if something happened to my own.

It was the first time that I experienced true mom fear.

Something changed inside of me that day. And every day since then, I have struggled with handing my children over to the Lord and entrusting them into his care. The question of "What if?" became my constant companion. When we went to the park, *What if someone would abduct my daughter?* When we went to the mall, *What if someone might have a gun and start shooting? What might happen if one of my kids got really sick?* When I would lie in bed at night, my mind would begin to race through every possible scenario of something bad happening to my baby. It got to the point that I was afraid to let my daughter out of my sight.

I decided that if I could always be with her and be in control of every situation, it would calm my heart and quiet the fears inside of my mind. And yet after months, and even years, of doing this same thing, I was still constantly asking, "What if?"

It's a trap that I think many of us fall into, and we don't even realize it. As mothers, we long to protect our children and keep them safe. But as I've continued to work through these fears over the years, I have found that there is really only one answer to all of the questions of "What if?"

We must choose to answer our fear with *"But God is..."* And then surrender to it.

Here's the thing about surrender, friend. It doesn't include contracts with God. Surrender doesn't include bartering. And ultimately, surrender means that we're not in control. Surrender means taking the thing that we fear the most and handing it over to God, no matter how much it scares us. Surrender is trusting that who God is will be enough for you, even if the what-ifs happen.

And who is God in light of fear? He is the opposite of fear: he is the shelter in my greatest storms. He is my peace.

In John 16:33, Jesus says, "I have said these things to you, that in me you may have peace. In the world you will have tribulation. But take heart; I have overcome the world." In this passage, Jesus is in the middle of saying goodbye to his disciples before his death on the cross—something that was going to cause more fear in their hearts than they had ever known. But even in his death, Jesus was wanting to reassure them of the peace that could be found in him. He doesn't tell them that everything is going to go well for them and that no troubles will come their way. No. In fact, he tells them, "In this world you *will* have troubles." That's a guarantee. But because they had surrendered their lives to him, because they chose to abide in him, they would receive his supernatural peace. And the same peace that Jesus promised his disciples that day he promises for you and me in the face of mom fear.

But how can peace in the midst of fear even be possible? Because he's already overcome the world! As Christians, we have peace with God, and our eternity is certain. Because of that we can have peace within our own minds and battle our fear at the foot of the cross in the protection of God's stability and everlasting love. Even when the what-ifs happen.

The fact is, fear is a hard thing to tackle. And I have to be honest, there are times that I have to give my fears over to God minute by minute because the grip that they have on my mind is so strong. But when I remember John 16:33 and remind myself of what God has overcome in the face of fear and in light of eternity, my fears are replaced with his peace.

Are trials going to come? Absolutely. Are painful things

going to happen to us? Of course. Are things that seem unimaginable going to be a part of our story? Because we live in a fallen world, the answer is yes. But because of the peace we have that is rooted in our faith in Christ, we can cling to the hope of eternity when the world is crumbling around us and the "What if?" questions consume our minds.

Take One Step into Peace:
Attack Your Fears

Once you have the foundation of trusting in what God has already done against evil according to Scripture, it makes it easier for you to attack your fears. The first thing you need to do today is to verbalize the fear you are experiencing and ask yourself a few questions about it. Is this fear realistic? It this fear imminent? What is the root of my fear?

Verbalizing your fears is one of the best ways to combat them. Sometimes when we say our fears out loud, we can recognize if they are or aren't realistic. No fear that you have is silly, but that doesn't mean that you need dwell on it. After answering these questions about your fear, you have two options: either act on that fear or pray on that fear. Some fears are very real and need action to ensure that they don't happen. But more often than not, our fears do not need to be acted upon, but rather prayed over. Asking someone to pray about those fears with you changes everything. Sit down with your husband or a trusted friend and share the fears you are experiencing. Talk through the questions that I listed above and be vulnerable. Take time to pray through these fears together and ask that person to help keep you accountable in handing your fears over to God. Remember, friend, you were never designed to face your fears alone! God created you for relationship and community. Not just with him, but with others as well.

Dear God,

Today I am struggling with fear. There are so many unknown things in motherhood that scare me, and I am unable to conquer these fears by myself. Oftentimes these fears make me feel like I am not enough and steal my peace. But God, I know that you are the opposite of fear. You are the refuge and safety I need! I trust that you will meet me when my fears are crippling and life doesn't make sense. Thank you for being a God we can come to when we are afraid, knowing that no fear is too big for you. In Jesus' name I pray,

Amen.

Day 16

WHEN JESUS COMMANDS US TO GO

*Go therefore and make disciples of all nations, baptizing them in the
name of the Father and of the Son and of the Holy Spirit, teaching them
to observe all that I have commanded you. And behold, I am with you
always, to the end of the age.*

MATTHEW 28:19—20

I think that the weeks surrounding Easter and Christmas can easily be the two weeks of the year that we talk about Jesus the most with our kids. Would you agree?

I remember when our oldest was about a year old; it was her first Christmas and I had this desperate desire for her to know the story of Jesus' birth because the holiday was close. It was like my motherhood was riding on her understanding it. I frantically sat down with her in front of the manger scene trying to explain the Christmas story to her. "This is Mary. Can you say Mary? And this is baby Jesus." I'm pretty sure, if my memory serves me right, that she picked baby Jesus up and threw him across the room. I was absolutely defeated, and I remember feeling like such a failure. Looking back, the whole scene was really quite ridiculous.

But let me ask you something serious. Are you *that desperate* to teach your children about Jesus the rest of the year? Are you pouring into the hearts of your kids when it isn't a Christian holiday? Do you get excited about sharing God's Word with your children?

I know that sometimes it can be easy to get complacent. I know that sometimes it gets lost in the shuffle of our busy lives. Once again, we fall into the trap of simply trying to keep up, and we forget that our simple moments of motherhood are our most sacred offerings when we allow them to be.

But we do forget, don't we, friend? We forget and then God gets forgotten except for two weeks of the year. Oftentimes, he is shoved to the back of those weeks by bunnies and a fat man in a red suit.

But what would happen if we invited God into the everyday with our kids? What if we invited him in to more of just praying at meals? What if our kitchen tables turned into a place of discipleship and our homes a place where his name is spoken daily? The fact is, discipleship isn't just an old word used in the Bible. It isn't just something that should be happening between adults. Discipleship is actually something that we should be doing in our day-to-day lives. The Bible calls us to it.

As Jesus was about to ascend into heaven, he gave very specific instructions to his disciples and to us. He commanded us to "Go . . . and make disciples of all nations, baptizing them in the name of the Father and of the Son and of the Holy Spirit, teaching them to observe all that I have commanded you." It is our calling to make disciples and spread the gospel. And for those of us who are mamas, the disciples we are called to make are the smallest of these. Deuteronomy 6:5–9 says,

You shall love the LORD your God with all your heart and with all your soul and with all your might. And these words that I command you today shall

be on your heart. You shall teach them diligently to your children, and shall talk of them when you sit in your house, and when you walk by the way, and when you lie down, and when you rise. You shall bind them as a sign on your hand, and they shall be as frontlets between your eyes. You shall write them on the doorposts of your house and on your gates.

Mamas, is there no greater calling in motherhood than to diligently make disciples of our children? Is there no greater purpose than to share the gospel with those whose lives we have been entrusted with? I think not.

I believe that one of the heaviest burdens that we carry as mothers is the spiritual well-being of our children. But often we feel unworthy of this calling, and it leads to fear. But as we discussed yesterday, God is the opposite of fear. He is peace! It is in trusting in the security of God that you will be able to disciple your children well and for his glory. I know that the responsibility of teaching your kids about God is a big one. I know that you might be sitting there saying, "I'm never going to be able to do this. I don't know enough about the Bible. I'm going to mess up every day. I don't think I'm qualified for this!" Here's the thing. You *aren't* going to do it perfectly. You *are* going to mess up. You *aren't* qualified. But God is. And just like we talked about last week, he will always meet you with wisdom when you ask for it.

God loves your children, and he has a plan for them and for their hearts. And aren't you just so glad that he chose you to be a part of it?

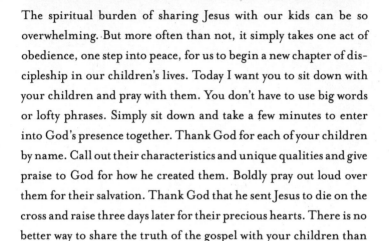

The spiritual burden of sharing Jesus with our kids can be so overwhelming. But more often than not, it simply takes one act of obedience, one step into peace, for us to begin a new chapter of discipleship in our children's lives. Today I want you to sit down with your children and pray with them. You don't have to use big words or lofty phrases. Simply sit down and take a few minutes to enter into God's presence together. Thank God for each of your children by name. Call out their characteristics and unique qualities and give praise to God for how he created them. Boldly pray out loud over them for their salvation. Thank God that he sent Jesus to die on the cross and raise three days later for their precious hearts. There is no better way to share the truth of the gospel with your children than through praising God and petitioning him in prayer.

Dear God,

I thank you for the gift of each of my children. I praise you for who you created them to be, in all of their uniqueness. But Lord, I want to lead them to you. Help me to be bold with my children in sharing your love with them. Give me opportunities to tell them about who you are and what your will is for their lives. Remind me that it is not my job to be their Holy Spirit, but help me to remember that it is my calling to lead them to it. I thank you that you have entrusted my kids to me. Help me to always remember to rely on you. In Jesus' name I pray,

Amen.

Day 17

WHEN YOU FIND YOURSELF IN SEASONS OF SACRIFICE

The heart of her husband trusts in her.

PROVERBS 31:11

It was eleven p.m. and I was just getting finished with the dishes from dinner. I was wiping down the countertops when I heard the crunch of the gravel underneath his truck tires. I walked to the door in time to see his headlights coming up over the hills of corn. It was harvest season for us, and eleven p.m. was actually getting in early for my husband during this time of the year.

Boy, had it been a day. My girls had been disasters from the moment they woke up, I had burned the lunch that I was supposed to bring out to the fields, I had laundry coming out of my ears, and I hadn't had a single moment alone in weeks. To make matters worse, I felt so incredibly lonely. We were only halfway through with harvest, and I was already running on empty. I had given so much of myself, and I was definitely going to let him hear all about it the moment my dear husband came through the door. Because really, what kind of stresses had he endured all day? What was it that he had given up? My anger was beginning to rise, and I was going to act on it.

I *deserved* to be able to take out my frustrations on him.

I wiped my hands on my apron and walked down the hallway toward him, ready to let him hear all about the misery of my day. But the closer I got to him, the more my heart softened. As I began to open my mouth, I paused. There stood my husband. He shut the door behind him and dropped his bags to the ground. He was covered in dust from hat to toe. He kicked off his shoes, removed his hat, and wiped his brow. He leaned back against the door and closed his eyes.

He was absolutely exhausted.

He looked over at me out of the corner of his eye; it was like he could hear the guilt creeping into my heart. I felt too ashamed to even approach him. He came walking down the hall toward me and wrapped his arms around my embarrassed frame. We stood there in that hallway and just held each other for a few minutes. "I love you," he whispered. How foolish I felt in that moment, foolish and fortunate. What a parody for this tired farmer's wife.

"I love you, too," I replied, tears streaming down my face. In that moment, something permanently shifted in my heart, all because my husband took the initial step to see the beauty in each of our sacrifices and lay down the weariness and emotions of the day. It completely humbled me.

I know I'm not the only one who's felt like this. We all have busy seasons in our families' lives. I know that there are so many other wives out there whose husbands work long hours or are gone on business trips many weeks of the year and they are left to hold down the fort at home. But isn't it during these times at home that we truly recognize the beauty in the hardship of sacrifice? And with that sacrifice comes trust—a trust that goes beyond the day in and day out, a trust that understands and *sees* one another's sacrifice with gratitude. For me, the sacrifice was in taking on all of the parenting roles alone, keeping the house running, and enduring a season of loneliness that came with my responsibilities. For him, the sacrifice was not just in the long hours but in the frustrations of machinery breakdowns, unpredictable weather, grain prices plummeting, and missing his family terribly. We each had our own burdens, but we had to choose to see the other's in light of our marriage as a whole.

Friend, we have the task of single-handedly being committed to our homes and our families during busy seasons in our families' lives. And while being faithfully committed in this way, we are also faithfully committed to our husbands during the busiest seasons of their lives and have the ability to give them trust with ease. *Trust extended to our spouse always gives way to peace between us.* May we continue to be trustworthy in seasons of sacrifice and be the wives that we have truly been called to be.

Take One Step into Peace:
Have a Vulnerable Conversation with Your Husband

During these busy times in the lives of our families, communication is often the first thing to slip away between husbands and wives. But it is also one of the first things to slip away between us and God. With our spouse, it can be so easy for us to assume that they know the hardship of our day or know what we need. It's an unfair expectation that we tend to set on our husbands, and when we remember that these types of expectations give way to chaos, we have to know that this only puts more pressure on both of us. Oftentimes, as wives we are so focused on the load we have on our own plates that we neglect to see or ask what our spouse is in need of. We must remember that communication with our husbands is everything during these seasons of sacrifice—this is a way that we can build a bridge of trust with them.

What I want you to do this evening after the kids are asleep is sit down and have a vulnerable conversation with your husband. Talk about your family's schedule for the rest of your week, ask him where he needs help, tell him where you need help, carve out some time that just the two of you can spend together, and honestly tell him how this season of life is making you feel. It's important to realize that not all of your requests to one another can be met, but at the very least you each know where the other is struggling and what their goals are. And sometimes simply hearing the other's mind is all that we need to have our hearts softened to theirs.

Loneliness is most likely going to be one of the emotions that you will bring up in your conversation with your spouse. Friend, this is when you must choose to lean into God. He *longs* to meet with you in these busy seasons of life, filling the void in your heart and restoring your peace. Let us not forget the promises we talked about on day 2, that God is always with you and that he is the strength of your heart and your portion. In allowing him to be that, the season of sacrifice will be less lonely and so much more holy.

Dear God,

I thank you for the gift of my marriage. In this busy season of raising our kids, it can be so hard for me to see the beauty in the chaos. But Lord, I long to serve my husband and children well. I know that I cannot do it without relying on your strength and being honest with my spouse. God, help me to press into your heart during this time in my life. Remind me that you desire to meet me when I am stressed and provide me with your strength and your peace. Likewise, when it can be so easy for me to be abrasive, help me to be a loving wife and press into my husband as well. God, may you soften my heart toward him and recognize the sacrifices we are both making. Help me to love him and offer understanding when he needs it most. Give us the time and opportunity to talk and keep the lines of communication open. It can be so overwhelming going through these years of our lives, but with you, we can walk through this season in confidence that you love us and have a plan for our marriage in it. Thank you for loving me and my husband. In Jesus' name I pray,

Amen.

Day 18

WHEN PRIDE KEEPS YOU FROM OPENING THE DOOR

A friend loves at all times,
and a brother is born for adversity.

PROVERBS 17:17

We had been in and out of doctors' offices for weeks: strep throat, ear infections, and now we were on the tail end of hand, foot, and mouth. *The horror.*

My oldest daughter, two and a half at the time, had been sitting in front of the television for three days straight as I tirelessly tried to sooth her sick baby sister. We were in the middle of planting, yet another season of sacrifice, and I had been all alone with two sick kids for weeks and had little to no help.

But here's the thing: people had *tried* to help. Friends had offered to drop off meals, and family had brought in groceries, asking if they could sit with the kids while I napped. But somewhere in my tired, I-have-to-pull-up-my-big-girl-panties mindset, I had said no to all of them.

Because of pride.

You see, one of the things that our culture today feeds women is that we are more than capable to do anything on our own. So much so that we have taken it to heart as mothers and we believe that there is no other way than to pull ourselves up and do it all by ourselves. We believe we are *weak* if we accept help. Even weaker if we ask for it.

I had been believing the lie of the big-girl panties again those last few weeks: the dishonest whispers in my ear that I had to handle this season by myself and not let anyone else into my mess. Because if I did that, I would look helpless and unworthy. "You don't need help," that serpent voice whispered into my heart. "You can't let anyone see you like this. What would they think of you if they saw how much you were struggling? Good moms could do this on their own."

But that day, oh that day, I was about to break and I knew I needed help. But we were all so close to being healthy again, so close to being out of our fever/incubation period, and I knew if I could just hang on a little bit longer that I could emerge victorious on my own.

That was when my doorbell rang.

Wait, who is that? Nobody asked if they could come over. What if they see how bad the house looks? I haven't showered in three days! I don't even have a shirt on, and I'm leaking milk through my bra. I can't open the door, I just can't, I thought as I scurried around trying to pick up dirty dishes while I bounced my screaming baby.

I walked over to the door and peered through the blinds. It was a friend from church; I didn't know her all that well, but she had always been so sweet when we had talked after the services. But there was no way she would ever be able to understand the mess I was in, no way I could hide my insecurities from her. My pride almost kept me from opening the door.

Almost.

The desperation inside of me won that day. When I opened

the door, she smiled and walked right in, the sound of my screaming baby not even seeming to faze her. She didn't look around the living room, or down at my shirtless chest, or at my sink full of dirty dishes, or even over at my daughter glued to the television. She looked me straight in the eyes and wrapped her arms around me in one of the most understanding hugs I've ever received. "I just wanted to tell you how loved you are, that you are a great mom, and you're doing such an incredible job. I'm not going to stay, but I needed to remind you that you aren't alone. This too shall pass, friend."

She handed me a card and a cup of coffee and scurried out the door, leaving me standing shirtless, dumbfounded, and utterly undone. Not undone because of my pride, but undone because in that moment, I was helped and allowed myself to be.

It was the most freeing moment of motherhood I had ever experienced.

Pride is such a tricky thing. More often than not, we view it as a positive attribute to have as a mom. But there's a much more stoic name we like to use for pride—we like to disguise it and call it "self-sufficiency." And while we are meant to rely on the Lord and his strength first and foremost as his child, we were also created to live in community with others. *God did not design us to carry our burdens on our own.* And, ultimately, pride isolates us within the insecurity of our own hearts and does not allow us to be met with friendship in our deepest times of adversity. Pride keeps us from experiencing relationships and keeps us away from vulnerability.

Friend, we must learn to humble ourselves, lay our pride aside, take off the big-girl panties, and allow ourselves to be helped. The kind of friendships that we truly long for will never come to fruition if we don't. Instead, our streak of lone-liness will continue, and we will isolate ourselves from the relationships that God designed us to be a part of, landing us right where the enemy wants us to be: feeling alone and stuck in our pride.

Take One Step into Peace:
Initiate Conversations

It can be so easy to feel like you are drowning in motherhood without friendship, and today we learned that pride is the number one thing that holds us back from grabbing the lifeline of other people. We long to be freed, yet continue deeper into the abyss of isolation by our own actions. But by initiating conversations with other women, we begin to break the chains of pride and open the door to vulnerability. For some of us, being the initiator can be a really hard thing, but I'm going to challenge you with it today.

Today, you are going to pick up your phone and call another woman and invite her over sometime this week. By simply putting yourself out there, you put yourself in the position to be vulnerable and allow someone else into your life. I know that it takes a lot to push that call button; I get it. But if it's your pride that's holding you back, then, girl, it's time to crush that pride with the punch of your thumb and the push of that green button.

Dear God,

Today I surrender my pride to you. I know that you did not design me to live a life dismantled by my self-made security, but one that is confident in your plan for my life and met by friendship with love.

I pray today, God, that you would humble my heart and let others into my life. Help me to be vulnerable in my own heart and honest in my conversations. And when help is offered to me when I need it most, I pray that you would remind me to accept it. In Jesus' name I pray,

Amen.

Day 19

WHEN YOU'RE ASKED TO PAY A PRICE

*Likewise, teach the older women to be reverent in the way they live, not
to be slanderers or addicted to much wine, but to teach what is good.
Then they can urge the younger women to love their husbands and
children, to be self-controlled and pure, to be busy at home, to be kind,
and to be subject to their husbands, so that no one will malign the word
of God.*

Titus 2:3–5 (niv)

I was really fortunate to have met Janet back before my husband
and I started having kids.

Janet was quite a bit older than me, but something clicked
between us and we hit it off right away. She seemed to know so
much about life and always had a wise word to share. You know
those kinds of people—she just oozed kindness and a quiet
confidence.

It was around the time that Janet and I met that I was working through one of the hardest seasons I had ever faced; my
heart was being held captive by so many emotions, but especially anger. When Janet found out how much I was struggling,
she invited me over for coffee one Saturday morning so that we
could spend some time talking about my where my heart was
and how I could move forward. Though I couldn't have known

in the moment, that one morning of coffee was the beginning of something so much more.

We entered into a season of discipleship.

We talked earlier this month about what it looks like to disciple our children: the intentional act of sharing the gospel with our kids and pointing them to Christ in everyday conversations. But how does it feel to be the one on the receiving end of hearing the gospel shared? What does it look like to be taught and learn how to walk with the Lord? The thing I love about God's plan for discipleship is that it looks different for everybody. But there is always one thing all discipleship relationships have: there is always a cost.

Obedience.

The price of discipleship is always obedience. Obedience to the commitment of time. Obedience to the commitment of sacrifice. Obedience to the commitment to be vulnerable. And ultimately, as women, the commitment to lay down our pride and be willing to learn what godly womanhood looks like. Because Janet was obedient to invest in my life and I was obedient to a willingness to be taught, we experienced the life-changing power of discipleship.

The apostle Paul addresses discipleship among women in the book of Titus, specifically about relationship between the older and younger women in the church and how crucial it is for us to become the women God longs for us to be.

But the sad thing is, I have seen young women dismiss the older women who have gone before them and the importance of these relationships Paul talks about. The younger women end up thinking that they are above the older women's wisdom and don't believe they need to hear how God changed their hearts and worked in their motherhood. These younger women believe that the story of the gospel worked out in the older women's lives does not apply to them. They let their pride keep them from being taught.

And unlike the day I almost didn't let my friend walk in the door because of my pride, in this case it is haughty pride that keeps us from walking through the door of discipleship. We have been fed the lies by our culture that we can handle it on our own as moms and that we don't need to be taught. That pride, that false sense of self-sufficiency, keeps us from being obedient in entering into discipleship, and it robs us of something so precious in our walk of motherhood. It's one of the most crucial mistakes our younger generation is making today.

For Janet and me, discipleship looked like sitting in her garden drinking coffee or going on walks through the woods at our local arboretum. Some days, it even looked like floating in her pool or sitting on her lounge chairs, wrapped up in wet towels for hours after we swam. But no matter where we were or what we were doing, God moved in our conversations. It never would have happened if we both hadn't chosen to show up and pay the price of discipleship: obedience.

Take One Step into Peace:
Find a Mentor

Finding a mentor can be an intimidating endeavor. Not only is finding someone who you think you can trust scary, but then reaching out and *asking* them to disciple you can be even scarier. But today you are going to start where all big steps of faith do:

reach out to God in prayer. Ask God to give you the opportunity to meet someone who can influence your life from the perspective of the Bible. Like we did last week when we prayed for your future friends, start praying for that person now, even though you don't know her by name yet. And pray for your own heart, too.

While discipleship leads to growth, it also causes you to look at your own life through the lens of Scripture. Ask God to start softening your heart to what your mentor wants to teach you and where God needs to transform your life. And ask that when God reveals the right person to you, you will both be ready and willing to pay the price of obedience in saying yes to discipleship.

Dear God,

I thank you that you have given me the desire to grow in my relationship with you. But I know that I need to take the next step in finding someone to disciple me and help me learn more about who you are and how I should use my motherhood to glorify you. I ask that you would bring someone into my life who is willing to invest in me, and that I would have the boldness to ask for their friendship in this way.

God, soften my heart to what my mentor will need to reveal to me; help me to have a teachable spirit and a humble mind. I trust that you are going to bring the right mentor to me, Lord. Thank you for your faithfulness in this already. In Jesus' name I pray,

Amen.

Day 20

WHEN IT'S TIME TO PUT DOWN THE MOP

Be merciful, even as your Father is merciful.

LUKE 6:36

Have you ever done one of those "See how your child responds" posts on Facebook? You know the ones: you give your child's name and age, then ask them a bunch of questions about you. Questions like "What is Mommy's favorite color?" or "Where does Mommy always go?" Or this one: "What does Mommy like to eat the most?" Both of my children answered, "Chipotle" on that one. I was so proud.

What can I say? They know their mama well.

But they also know me well enough to have answered some of the other questions honestly, too. It was their answers to these questions that completely changed how I spend my time with them and where my priorities lie.

One of the questions was "What is something Mommy always does?" I had seen so many other parents' kids' responses and figured that mine would be the same, too. A lot of kids had responded with "My mommy plays with me" or "My mommy gets me snacks." But my kids? My kids both answered that their mommy "cleans all the time."

Truth be told, yes. As a stay-at-home mom, my kids see me do a lot of cleaning. Taking care of all five of us, plus making three meals (and a million snacks) a day calls for a lot of mess making and mess cleaning up.

But it was the next question that completely broke my heart. "What is something that your mommy always says to you?" Like clockwork, no hesitation, both of my girls responded, "Stop making a mess. I just cleaned that."

If there has been one moment that has brought me more conviction in motherhood than any other one, it was this. Of all the things that I tell my children through the day—that I love them, that they look beautiful, that their drawings look pretty, that I'm proud of them, that God loves them, that they do a good job—of all the things they could have said, the first thing that came to their minds was that they were messing up something that was more important to me than they were.

And in the words of John Trainer, "Children are not a distraction from more important work. They are the most important work."

I get it. I know that we all have things that need to get done around the house. I know people need to eat and babies have to be fed and everyone needs to have clean underwear. But how often are we choosing to put the housework ahead of the condition of our children's precious hearts? Are we cultivating environments of love and play, or are we picking apart every tiny spill and mess they make? It's time to take a stand against perfectionism in our homes and choose to meet our children with mercy that only the Father can supply us with.

Here's the thing about trying to keep the house perfect, friend. It's the number one unrealistic expectation we set as moms that causes us the most stress. It sets the stage for a false sense of reality and feeds us the lie that what we do in our homes

has to be without fault. But when we meet the lie of perfectionism with the freedom of mercy and remember that God's only
expectation of us is to be obedient in striving for more of him,
we can confidently set the mop in the corner and let it be.

God cares about the messiness of your heart more than the
messiness of your floors, sweet mama. And he cares about the
mercy you extend to your kids more, too.

Take One Step into Peace:
Leave One Thing Undone Today

It can be so overwhelming when we look at everything we have
to do around the house, can't it? But today I want you to pick
one thing and leave it undone. Leave a load of laundry in the
dryer, don't empty the dishwasher, leave the toys scattered
on the floor, or don't sweep up the crumbs for the tenth time
today. Sit on the couch and invite your kids up into your lap or
to sit next to you. Ask them what their favorite part of their day
was or one thing that made them smile. Take this time to pray
over your kids like we talked about earlier this month. Invest
the time that you would have put into your house into intentional moments with your children today.

Dear God,

I am so grateful that you have provided me with a house to care for and children to raise. Sometimes the needs of both of them overwhelm my mind and I find myself putting the needs of my house before my kids. I know that this is not how my priorities should be. Help me to not be so consumed with taking care of my home that I miss opportunities to love my children well and extend them your mercy. Equip me with patience when they make a mess and mercy when I don't think that I have any left, especially at the end of the day. I don't want to fall into the trap of letting my emotions dictate my actions. Thank you for going before me, God. In Jesus' name I pray,

Amen.

Day 21

WHEN YOU FEEL DEFEATED AT CHURCH

And day by day, attending the temple together and breaking bread in
their homes, they received their food with glad and generous hearts,
praising God and having favor with all the people. And the Lord added
to their number day by day those who were being saved.

ACTS 2:46—47

There I found myself, being that mom in the pew again, the one who was interrupting the service, dragging out her two small toddlers (who were begging for fruit snacks) while bouncing the baby, flinging an oversized diaper bag over her shoulder, and shoving her rear in everyone's face as she shuffled down the pew aisle. Yep, that was me. And it was just another Sunday at church for me and my ragamuffin crew.

Sound familiar?

I think that one thing we can all agree on is that while we know it's worth the effort to get the kids dressed for church and out the door (just to hear half the sermon and leave five minutes early because of a massive blowout), most young families who attend church come to be fed and encouraged but often leave feeling defeated and lonely. And what's worse is that the stronghold of discouragement clutches them so tightly that they give up going to church altogether, promising to start attending again when the kids are older and they get a little easier.

I completely understand. My husband and I have been there. *We're still there.* And chances are that you are, too. So, since we're all in the same season of waiting for things to get "easier," can I share something that has drastically changed the way that we as a family connect with people at church?

Small groups.

I'm pretty sure that every church has a different name for it. Some call it Bible study. Some call it life groups, connect groups, or couples' study. But it all means the same thing: families getting together in one another's houses in the name of Jesus and doing life together. It isn't necessarily "easier," but I'll tell you what it does bring to the table:

Consistency.

Vulnerability.

Authenticity.

Friendship.

Accountability.

It almost always includes dessert.

And trust. Not just trust in one another, but trust in the One who called us together for his purpose and for our growth in him.

I'm not sure if you noticed as you were reading through the list above, but aren't so many of those things what we *crave* in our relationships? Gospel-centered community enriches our lives in ways that we can't even begin to imagine, friend. This isn't a bunch of people sitting around in a dimly lit room and praying in silence. For our families, this is ten adults sitting on couches and on the floor with Bibles open and hearts yearning for truth, and it's twelve kids flinging Goldfish like confetti, running room to room, and constantly being told to "Go back into the bedroom and give us five more minutes." It's being honest when we don't understand something that Scripture says and being even more honest when we struggle with how it convicts us. It's holding one another when life gets hard and jumping up and down when we see the victories that we've prayed about for so long together become reality. It's bearing one another's burdens and committing to pray for them during the week. And it's looking across the room and seeing someone understanding Scripture for the very first time.

God didn't intend church to be confined to the walls of its building. Acts 2 tells us very clearly that the people of the early church met in the temple *and* in their homes; hearts were changed in both places! This is community the way God intended it to be! For us to "consider how to stir up one another to love and good works, not neglecting to meet together, as is the habit of some, but encouraging one another, and all the more as you see the Day drawing near" (Hebrews 10:24–25). For us to raise our families in Christ, not just in the church. And for us to raise them together, not alone.

Take One Step into Peace:
Get Plugged In

If you find yourself longing for a sense of belonging in your church, chances are that it can be hard to find your place within the body without getting involved deeper than Sunday mornings. But that can all change with one phone call today. If a Bible study community is something that you don't have in your life, I want you to pick up the phone and call your church.

Ask them what types of small groups or Bible studies they have available, decide as a couple which one you want to try, and get plugged in. It can be so scary to show up to someone's house for the first time in a big group (it's like junior high all over again). But that step of boldness is one that you must take if you want to experience true community the way God longs for you to.

I know that for some of you this is a hard subject to tackle if your husband does not attend church or does not want to be involved in one. It is still so important that you offer for him to be involved in this process, even if you think he will say no. Not including him not only doesn't give him the chance to say yes to something new, but it also doesn't give you an opportunity to have an influence on his heart. I Peter 3:1 says, "Likewise, wives, be subject to your own husbands, so that even if some do not obey the word, they may be won without a word by the conduct of their wives." As a spouse, you have an unbelievable opportunity to be a witness to your husband, friend. Don't let your fear of him saying no hold you back from inviting him in.

God created you for community, friend, community that will encourage your heart and community that will give you the friendships you desire. Don't waste another day living on the outside of one. It's time to get plugged in today.

Dear God,

Thank you for giving me the longing to be part of a community of believers. But sometimes just going to church on Sundays isn't enough, and I am often discouraged during this season of my life. I ask that you would give me the courage to call my church or someone I know who loves you and help me join a small group. After today, I realize that I need more consistent accountability and vulnerability in my life and in our family, and I trust that you are going to bring the right Bible study into my life. I pray that my husband and I would feel comfortable in the group you lead us to, growing us in our faith both separately and together. We will wait expectantly as you show us which direction to go next. In Jesus' name I pray,

Amen.

Day 22

WHEN MAMA GETS HER FEELINGS HURT

Let all bitterness and wrath and anger and clamor and slander be
put away from you, along with all malice. Be kind to one another,
tenderhearted, forgiving one another, as God in Christ forgave you.

EPHESIANS 4:31–32

I've had a lot of friendships come and go over the years. Some changed when we moved away, some because the seasons of life shifted for one or both of us, and some simply because we drifted apart. But I think the friendships that have ended abruptly in hurt feelings have been the ones that sting the most. The intense feelings that were associated with their ending still make my heart cringe and find me wishing that I could have done things better—that I would have been brave enough to sift through my emotions, working toward reconciliation instead of being controlled by my hurt feelings and running in retreat.

So instead of running away from these big feelings, we must ask ourselves how we can do better on our end when we get our feelings hurt. While it isn't our job to work through the feelings in somebody else's heart, it is our job to take responsibility for what's in ours. And more often than not, it starts with allowing ourselves to feel all the feels.

I don't know about you, but the phrase "get over it" does not sit well with me. But it is usually the first thing I tell myself when

I've been hurt (another lie of the big-girl panties). It causes me to cage my emotions, making me feel trapped and isolated, and it blurs the truth that I'm trying to come to grips with. The longer I try to push these feelings down, the more ashamed of them I feel, knowing in my heart that I'm doing more harm to myself, and the person who hurt me, than good. Instead, I should be allowing myself to come face to face with the pain inside. And while the release of emotion is healthy, living in these emotions for any prolonged period of time is not.

This is when we entrust our feelings over to the One who created us to experience emotion in the first place.

Take a Few Steps into Peace:
Seek Reconciliation

Notice that I'm not just asking you to take one step into peace today. I'm asking you to take a few. Because more often than not, getting to a place of peace with our hurt feelings takes more than just one step.

Whether you believe that reconciliation with your friend is possible or not, you must not put your emotions into the glass cases. If you do, they are just going to continue to grow, clouding your ability to see you as God does and inhibiting you from entering into healthy friendships down the road. This might be the hardest part, but it is also the most necessary—today, you need to start with the prayer below before you move any further.

I'm going to be honest with you: it's going to seem a little bit foggy when you first start; it's going to seem like you will never be rid of these feelings of betrayal. But take heart: God is getting ready to do something beautiful in your soul, friend! But he can't do that if you aren't surrendering your feelings to him first.

Pray that your heart would be granted peace and your mind clarity. Ask that you would be quick to listen and slow to speak. And while you're at it, pray for the friend who hurt your heart.

When you feel like you have come to a place where your emotions aren't so intense, it's time to talk it out. Sitting across the table and looking someone in the eye who has hurt you is a painful thing. But the Lord goes before you in this conversation, friend! Whether you have this conversation alone or with another trusted friend, be sure to speak in love and truth as well as be a listener in grace. You must give your friend space to be able to share her heart as you have shared yours. You might not come to a place of reconciliation in this conversation, but it's the first step toward healing—for both of you.

While every outcome is different, I do know that when you come to a place when you are ready to forgive as God calls us to, it's going to be a choice of love first. Just like God loves you and has forgiven you for the wrongs you have done against him, God loves your friend just the same. And as followers of Jesus, it is our desire to chase after his character so that it is manifested in us. His character is one of forgiveness. And forgiveness always gives way to peace. "And the peace of God, which surpasses all understanding, will guard your hearts and your minds in Christ Jesus" (Phil. 4:7).

Dear God,

Today I am struggling with hurt feelings from a friend. God, you know what is going on and see me in these emotions. I so badly want to be freed from them. But now I know that I can't do that without surrendering them to you. I hand my emotion of _____ over to you right now. God, please allow my heart to be softened to my friend who has done this to me. Help me to love her as you do, with a heart of mercy and forgiveness. I know that you are a God of restoration, and I pray that today you would honor my obedience and make a way for this friendship to be redeemed. I believe that you will go before me! When I meet with her next, please empower me with your strength and a calm heart, willing to talk and listen in your love. Thank you so much for loving me, God. I lay my heart at your feet today. In Jesus' name I pray,

Amen.

Day 23

WHEN YOU'RE GIVEN THE CHOICE TO GET IN

Therefore I tell you, do not be anxious about your life, what you will eat or what you will drink, nor about your body, what you will put on it. Is not life more than food, and the body more than clothing?

MATTHEW 6:25

It had been on my mind for most of the week. When I found out that our family had been invited to a pool party, my first thought was to shut the idea down as fast as the invitation had come. It was hard enough for me to take all three of my kids anywhere, but the pool was an entirely different story. Not just because the kids were difficult, but because going to the pool made me difficult, too. I think you already know where I'm going with this.

We got to the party and my kids ran right into the pool, joining the other kids already in the water. The parents all stood along the side of the pool, talking and watching the kids playing. Before too long, all of the kids were begging their parents to come in, trying to coax them by splashing water their way. One by one, we all gave our kids excuses as to why we wouldn't get in, watching their little disappointed faces as they swam back out into the water.

I sat there and fidgeted under my cover-up, knowing that pretty soon it would be my own kids begging me to come in and play. And once my middle daughter's eyes caught mine, I knew it was my time to give an answer. "Mommy! Mommy! Come play with me!" she cried out, as she spat water out of her mouth. And in that moment, my daughter gave me a choice. She gave me the choice to sit on the sidelines in my insecurity or to get over myself and *get in*.

Going to the pool can be such a hard thing for us moms, let alone finding a suit we feel beautiful and confident in. The insecurity we tend to feel about our post-baby bodies can be so consuming that it easily takes away one of the most joyful gifts that we get to experience with our kids—the gift of play. I don't know about you, but it can be consuming enough that I find myself sick with anxiety any time I know I'm going to be seen in my bathing suit in the near future. To me, my size more than matters.

Here's the thing, mamas. Our kids are only this little for this short amount of time. They're only going to beg for us to get in and be a part of their world for only so long. And why should we spend the years of their littleness sitting on the sidelines in the insecurity of our mom bods, rather than being fully present in the moment and choosing to get in?

I don't know about you, friend, but I don't want to look back ten years from now and wish that I could have jumped in just one more time. And oh my goodness, I don't want to look back in regret and realize just how many memories the insecurity about my body stole from me.

No. More. Memories. Stolen. Mama. Your heart is too precious to let these moments keep passing you by.

And in case you were wondering, I took the cover-up off. I got in the pool that night. My kids jumped off the side and into my arms, I gave them piggyback rides, we splashed water into each other's faces, and we laughed our heads off. I didn't let my size matter, because when I live in the moment with my kids, I'm a size mom. And it's the most perfect size I could ever want to be.

Take One Step into Peace:
Play Today

There's a good chance that on the day you're reading this, you won't be going to the pool with your kids. But if I would have to guess, I bet that today you will play with your kids, maybe even out in public or around friends. Here's what I want you to do before you play with them: don't think about it. Before you walk out onto that playground, don't cinch up your pants and keep making sure that every roll is tucked perfectly into place. As you get down on the floor, really get down on the floor, roll around, crawl on your hands and knees. Don't worry if anyone is noticing the parts of you that you're insecure about. And if you do get into that pool, I beg you with everything in me, *jump in*. Jump in and make a splash. Jump in and lock eyes with your kids while you do it. I promise, looking at the joy on their faces is just so much better than worrying about how you look while you're doing it. You are a beautiful gift, mama friend. Don't be afraid to get in today.

Dear God,

I am so thankful that I have the ability to play with my children and I am so grateful that they still want to play with me. But God, there are times when I let my insecurity hold me back from getting in and truly being involved in playing with them. In fact, there have been so many things that I have missed out on, simply because I have been too worried about what others might think about how I look. But God, you see me as a loving mother, and my kids see me as the best mom ever. Help me to remember that today is the only one of its kind and that I will never have this day with my kids again. Help me to choose moments of presence instead of moments of embarrassment. Remind me that I am loved and valued by you! In Jesus' name I pray,

Amen.

Day 24

WHEN MOTHERHOOD BECOMES YOUR GIFT

Each of you should use whatever gift you have received to serve others,
as faithful stewards of God's grace in its various forms. If anyone
speaks, they should do so as one who speaks the very words of God. If
anyone serves, they should do so with the strength God provides, so that
in all things God may be praised through Jesus Christ. To him be the
glory and the power for ever and ever. Amen.

1 Peter 4:10–11 (niv)

I've always been so surprised at the conversations I have with my kids in the car. We were driving on our way to dance a few weeks ago and somehow the girls and I got started talking about glorifying God with our gifts. I explained to them that when God made them, he did everything on purpose. He made them to do all kinds of things well, and that even the smallest of gifts can be used to glorify God when we rely on his strength to do them. Even the gifts that they use when nobody notices. My middle child, just three years old, piped up in the back seat, "Mommy! What are my gifts?"

"Well," I said with a chuckle, "He made you to be a good artist, to make people laugh, to be a hard worker, and to be strong and fast. And honey, all of those things are great, but doing them for God gives you a greater reason to do them well. Honoring God is the greatest thing you can ever do with the gifts he has given you. And he made you pretty special."

A few minutes passed and she piped up again, "Mom, you have gifts!"

"Oh, yeah, what are some of Mommy's gifts?" I thought maybe she would say that I cook good food, that I'm a silly dancer, or that I am a good tickler (I've always prided myself on that). But what she said next took my breath away.

"You come get me in my room when I call for you at night," she said matter-of-factly. "That makes God happy."

Immediately I felt a lump in my throat and tears started to well up in my eyes. "Yes, baby. Getting up with you in the middle of the night is one of my gifts. And using that gift brings God so much joy." That day on our way to dance class, God used my daughter to give my heart the validation that I had been seeking but had been looking for in all the wrong places. I was longing to be applauded in my motherhood by the world, only to realize that the One who sees me offers the applause that matters most.

We live in a world that longs to be seen and noticed, cheered for and praised. And mama friend, if you're reading this right now, it might be hard to see what you do in the everyday mundane as your gift when nobody is applauding you. Nobody cheers for the all-nighters you pull or the hours you spend playing trucks on the floor or the countless sibling fights you break up. And I know that nobody cheers for you as you get up day after day, night after night, strength or no strength, and give your kids everything you've got.

But that is your gift. The gift of your hidden self. The gift of quiet servanthood.

What you do in these hours that nobody else sees—it matters to him. And it matters to the little people who call out your name in the middle of the night, too.

Take One Step into Peace:
Validate Others

Chances are you are going to get called out of bed tonight. And chances are you might bemoan having to answer that call. But before you fall asleep tonight, I want you to ask God to bless the midnight hours of service to your family. Ask him to remind you that you have the opportunity to use your gift well and with an attitude of joy, even when nobody else sees. Not only that, but ask him to reveal to you some of the other gifts that you have found in motherhood. God longs to be able to take our strengths and use them for his great purposes, and for us to find joy in them.

The next thing you get to do with this truth today is to share it with another mama friend. When you talk to her today, point out one thing that you've noticed is her gift as a mom and remind her that her gifts are seen, not just by you, but by the God who designed her with them. Validating other women and empowering them to be all that they are in Christ is hands down the best thing we can do for our friends.

Dear God,

Sometimes in motherhood it is hard to find what I am good at. It's difficult to find my strengths and be able to be proud of who I am becoming. But God, you see the everyday things that I do and call them my gifts. Even more, you delight in the things that are unseen by everyone else and call those the greatest gifts of all. Would you help me to be able to see that tonight? As I get up in the middle of the night to serve my children, remind me of the purpose found in these gifts and that you long to see me use them. As I get up with my children tonight, help me to have an attitude that is a reflection of your peace. Let the words of my mouth and the meditations of my heart bring you glory as I serve my children. In Jesus' name I pray,

Amen.

Day 25

WHEN YOU FORGET HOW TO BE A BRIDE

But from the beginning of creation, "God made them male and female." "Therefore a man shall leave his father and mother and hold fast to his wife, and the two shall become one flesh." So they are no longer two but one flesh. What therefore God has joined together, let not man separate.

MARK 10:6–9

I remember the day that my husband first suggested that we leave our oldest daughter with one of our moms and go out of town for the weekend together. She was nine months old, and I was terrified.

What if the baby gets sick while I'm gone?

What if something happens to me while I'm gone?

What if she won't take her bottle?

What if we leave and I can't have fun being away from her?

What if her grandma doesn't apply the right amount of Butt Paste when she changes her diaper?

What if she doesn't remember me when I get home?

Did you notice that I didn't mention my husband in any of those questions? Yeah, that was the problem. I had become so wrapped up in being a mom that I had completely forgotten what it was like to be a bride.

My husband and I always told one another that we wouldn't let ourselves get lost in the trenches of parenthood, that having kids wouldn't change us, and that we wouldn't forget the sense of togetherness that we clung to in our early years of marriage. They were really well-intentioned promises, honestly. And I think that they came from hearts that truly wanted to keep their word. But babies don't come with an agreement to help you keep those promises. And they certainly don't come with a handbook, either. Luckily for us, marriage actually does.

One of the biggest pitfalls that couples fall into today is that they allow their children to take the place of each other. I'm not just talking about co-sleeping or giving a little too much attention here; I'm talking rock-your-marriage, steal-your-relationship, put-the-children-in-front-of-the-other marriage crumbler. We give the excuse that it's just the season of life that we're in or that we're too tired to put in the effort because our kids have already taken all of it. Or the biggest one, that one day we will have more time for one another. I'm calling our bluff, friend. I'm calling our bluff and I'm telling you that we've been wrong.

The place we put our children in comparison to our spouses is silently killing our marriages, and we don't even know it! The excuses we create slowly bury us in a hole that we've dug for ourselves. And the saddest thing is, we've dug the hole big enough for two, and we lead our husbands right down into it beside us.

God joined you and your husband together, friend. He joined you together, and he intends for you to stay that way.

But in the midst of parenthood, in the messiness of being a mom, and in the sifting through of the emotions of your precious heart, don't forget that you were a bride first and a mama second. Children are the greatest gift that can come from our marriages, but only because you gave the gift of yourselves to each other first.

So, go ahead, mama. Take that trip. Fix your hair up. Go on that date. Flirt with your husband. Hold his hand. Kiss his lips. And for heaven's sake, get frisky in the kitchen. And take time to tell him you love him. Look into his eyes and cherish the gift that he is. Remember the plan that God has in the beauty of your marriage. And don't forget that what God joined together no man, or child, should separate.

Take One Step into Peace:
Invest in Your Husband

I think it's easy for all of us to see how motherhood has affected our marriages, positively and negatively. But sometimes we don't even realize how far we have slipped away from each other or how much we have allowed our kids to come in between us.

Today I want you to think of something that makes you feel like being a wife and do it: rest your arm on your husband's leg, cuddle up next to him on the couch, throw your arms around his neck and give him a flirty kiss...Ask him on a date! I know it's going to take some effort. I know that you might not feel like doing it. And I know that maybe your kids might even see. But taking the time to invest in your husband with the best of your efforts and the heart of a bride will go a long way. You never know how one step of intentional intimacy will shift both of your perspectives off of the kids and back onto each other. Every moment in our marriages counts, friend. Make the most of them today.

Dear God,

You have blessed us so greatly with the gift of our family; I am so thankful for each and every one! But because I am needed in so many ways by all of them, it is hard to remember to give my husband the attention he needs and deserves. God, I pray that you would give me the moments I need to be able to be intentional and present with my husband today. Help me to remember the love and affection I have for him and help me to take the time to show it to him. My husband is such a gift to me, and I thank you for him. Help me to show him how I feel today. In Jesus' name I pray,

Amen.

Day 26

WHEN MAMA GETS SICK

God is our refuge and strength,
a very present help in trouble.
Therefore we will not fear though the earth gives way,
though the mountains be moved into the heart of the sea,
though its waters roar and foam,
though the mountains tremble at its swelling. Selah.

PSALM 46:1–3

Have your kids ever had hand, foot, and mouth? Neither of mine had ever had it before, and when it hit our house, I was convinced that all was lost. Not only were my kids writhing in pain with their little bodies covered in sores and all of their fingernails and toenails peeling off, but they had just gotten over strep throat two weeks prior, and I had the worst sinus infection of all time. Sickness had hit our house in full force; we were paying doctor's office copays out our ears, and no matter how much my sweet husband tried to help, the only person that my babies wanted was their mama.

But mama doesn't get sick days, does she, friend? Mama doesn't get to go home and curl up in bed and take the day off. And mama certainly doesn't get a Netflix marathon and chicken noodle soup delivered to her bedside, either.

Sickness can single-handedly be one of the most debilitating, defeating parts about motherhood, especially when sickness in your house goes on for weeks on end. Not only is it hard to watch your kids feel so terrible and then feel that way yourself, but sickness for extended periods like that isolates you from everyone else and makes you feel like you are about to lose your ever-loving mind. And over time that isolation drains you. No longer is it just your physical strength failing, but your emotional strength begins to dwindle, too. And from the first moment that you hear that middle-of-the-night cough or those heaves coming from the room down the hallway, your heart becomes a ticking time bomb, and the enemy knows it.

But that is when God steps in and he becomes our source of strength when we allow him to, mama friend. Sometimes it takes us coming to the most desperate places of motherhood to realize that it is only by his strength alone that we can get through the next day, hour, or even minute. Some days it feels like the earth is about to give way. Some weeks it feels like you are going to drown in the exhaustion of motherhood. But God's strength is greater; his endurance in you is enough to sustain you in seasons of sickness. And speaking this verse over your body and your household will empower you more than you know. Because this verse is the deliverance of peace in your time of trouble.

For me this was the verse I prayed as I hung my head over the toilet in my three pregnancies. It was the verse I prayed while I rocked teething babies in the middle of the night. It was this verse I prayed as I sat my girls in my lap and read them books during the December when we all had the flu. This was the verse I whispered as I slipped in and out of consciousness while I bled on the operating table as they pulled our youngest from my womb.

And this is the verse that will bring you the peace of Jesus and the strength of his mighty hand to weather the storm of sickness in your house, sweet friend. His strength will always be more than enough for you when you call on his name. Keep clinging to it, and he will be faithful to deliver his strength to you.

Take One Step into Peace:
Ask for His Strength

So often, it takes us getting to our most physically and mentally drained to become desperate for God and his endurance. But when we practice it in the everyday mundane moments, we are already one step ahead of the game and we go into days of sickness in our homes armed with his power already working in us. So, before you have another episode like that in your house, let's practice depending on God's strength today. When you feel like you are beginning to grow tired or your patience low with your kids, pray this verse over your heart. Trust that God will sustain you and empower you with his strength. Strength from above is not that of your own, friend; it's supernatural, and you don't have to come up with it by yourself. But you do need to ask for it.

Dear God,

   I am so thankful that you are a God who empowers me with your strength when I call on your name. Would you grant me your strength today as I mother my kids? Give me energy to be able to be present with my children and get done what I need to today. I pray a prayer of health over myself and my family; keep them safe and healthy, protected under your wings. God, I know that it is only a matter of time before someone does get sick. When that time comes, help me to remember your promises for me—that you will sustain me and be my strength when I feel like I can't go on any longer. Thank you for being a God who meets me when I am at my weakest. In Jesus' name I pray,

Amen.

Day 27

WHEN YOU PARENT WITH SHAME

The LORD is merciful and gracious,
slow to anger and abounding in steadfast love.
He will not always chide,
nor will he keep his anger forever.
He does not deal with us according to our sins,
nor repay us according to our iniquities.
For as high as the heavens are above the earth,
so great is his steadfast love toward those who fear him;
as far as the east is from the west,
so far does he remove transgressions from us.

PSALM 103:8–12

One of the most intense emotions that has an effect on how we raise our kids is the fear of who our children will one day become in light of how we parent them. It's a powerful stronghold that the enemy uses to sway our hearts as we learn how to raise our children, often leading us to discipline them into action rather than a change of heart toward obedience in Christ. And it was this fear that led me to one of the most painful lessons that I've had to learn as a parent, one that has shaped my heart the most as I've learned how to discipline my kids.

I'm not sure about you, but it's hard for me to see the lack of respect in some of our young people today: kids walking all over their parents, parents not being firm enough in their discipline, and in the end children not having a realistic grasp of authority. When my daughter was about two years old and her disobedient heart began to emerge, I vowed that she would never be "one of *those* kids." It put such a strong fear in my heart as a mom, a fear that, for a time, I thought was simply a healthy motherly instinct that I needed to follow. But remember what fear does? It crumbles you from the inside out and distorts your sense of reality.

You see, one of the things that I long for the most for my kids is for them to have a strong sense of conviction at an early age, a clear understanding of right and wrong in light of God's Word, so that as they get older it will be that much easier for them to resist the temptations of this world and make decisions that honor Jesus. But it was in this desire for them to make wise choices and my fear for them to be disciplined too delicately that Satan crept into my parenting right under my nose. And slowly, the discipline I gave my daughter became simply about her actions rather than the obedience of her heart.

It all started out so innocently. *The more I repeat myself, the better chance she has of not forgetting my words. She needs to remember that I'm the one in charge,* I would tell myself as I disciplined her. My daughter would disobey a simple instruction, and I would scold one too many times, explaining that poor actions always have repercussions, then giving her a consequence. But it didn't stop there. Soon it grew into hanging her disobedience over her head, reminding her long after her initial scolding how naughty she had been. My words became increasingly harsh and my tone more intense, and any amount of compassion I had was gone. And ultimately, my discipline turned into soul shaming rather than nurturing heart work. I had fallen down a slippery slope, and my well-intentioned heart had given way to something far more powerful, far more vicious, than anything I would ever have imagined it could be. This often left my daughter crying in her room, hiding from her mommy, who didn't know when enough was enough. The very memory of those tears streaming down her face as she sat on her closet floor breaks my heart to this day.

While kids need sternness, they also need compassion. And the compassionate molding of our children's hearts should always take precedence over a momentary loss of our emotions that gives way to disciplining them into humiliation. Shame tells them that our love for them is conditional. Shame makes our children feel isolated. Shame unnecessarily reminds them of their faults and causes chaos in their tiny minds. And ultimately, shame tells them that they are not enough.

And our precious children... oh, they are more than enough, friend. Our kids are *worthy* of their parents disciplining them with the heart of the Father, who is both loving and just. But justice must always be led by love. Because if we don't remember that, we are going to crush our children's spirits, one moment of discipline at a time, leaving them to pick up all the broken pieces by themselves.

I learned my lesson early. I was able to tame the beast of shaming inside of me, but it was not without consequences. Both of us crumbled under the pressure of the shame that I put on her. I was able to ask for and receive forgiveness from my daughter, but we have had to work through the hurt that I have caused her delicate little heart, and I have had to work through the regret I have because of it. Each day that part of my parenting continues to be redeemed and our relationship restored, but wow, I wish that didn't have to be.

You don't have to go down that road any further than you already have today, friend. Today you can stop the cycle of shaming and enter back into parenting in peace.

I want you to take a look back at how you have disciplined your kids over the last twenty-four hours and see if there was a time that you shamed your child. It can be easy to miss if you have been caught in its trap for too long; I know it took time for me to be able to recognize it. But if we don't catch it soon enough, we can easily hurt our children's hearts more than we realize. If you have done that today, I want you to go to your child and ask for forgiveness. You have a beautiful opportunity to show your children humility today in pointing out your own wrongdoing and asking them for forgiveness for disciplining them with shame. And ultimately, you have the chance to direct them to the heart of God, who is merciful and gracious, slow to anger, and abounding in steadfast love.

Dear God,

Today I have seen my sin in how I discipline my children. I have been trying to make them obey out of shame instead of pointing them to a heart of obedience and repentance. But Lord, today I ask for your forgiveness. Cleanse me of my lack of compassion and fill me with your mercy for my kids. Help me to discipline in firmness, but to lead in love, just as you have done with me. Thank you so much for your forgiveness in my life, God. Today, I walk in your forgiveness and love for me! In Jesus' name I pray,

Amen.

Day 28

WHEN YOU BELIEVE WHO REGRET SAYS YOU ARE

Not that I have already obtained this or am already perfect, but I press on to make it my own, because Christ Jesus has made me his own. Brothers, I do not consider that I have made it my own. But one thing I do: forgetting what lies behind and straining forward to do what lies ahead. I press on toward the goal for the prize of the upward call of God in Christ Jesus.

PHILIPPIANS 3:12–14

It was when I finally recognized just how much I had forced my daughter into a place of shame that I began to feel that same humiliation in my own heart as well. I had asked her for forgiveness and I had sought out the same from God, but what I was left with was a heart of regret, trapped in my own hole of mom shame.

I entered into a season of self-doubt that made me question every move I made with my kids, and even with my husband. The words *I'm sorry* became my constant companion. Not out of a heart of repentance, but out of a place of regret, fearing that I was once again doing everything wrong. I was so afraid of making the same mistakes over again that I didn't know how to move forward or find a place of peace in my heart. And what I was ultimately doing was holding God's grace at an arm's length from my own heart and allowing the shame of my decisions to control my every move.

As moms, we have to recognize that we aren't perfect; we're going to make mistakes. There are going to be lapses in our judgment and errors in how we parent our kids. And gosh, we are going to be convicted by the Spirit and our hearts will be broken by it. But we must remember that as we are to extend the grace and forgiveness of God to our children in their mistakes, we must extend it to ourselves as well. Recognizing our mistakes is one thing, but living in the regret of them is another. And if God calls us to press on toward the purification of Christ and the perfection of his character, then regret is only going to hold us back from everything that God has for us, especially in motherhood.

Here's the thing, friend. Regret only shows me where I've gone wrong and ignores how far God has brought me. Regret squelches my confidence and tells me that God can't use me any longer. Regret leads to a heart set in chaos and emptied of peace. And living in that regret always leads to shame.

But a woman who is empowered by the truth that she is known and loved by God in spite of her mistakes, in spite of her flaws, and in spite of her sin? That woman is one who lives a fulfilled life found in the forgiveness of the cross, at peace in the plan of the Father and confident that he is continuing a good work in her.

Is it not worth the risk to feel uncomfortable for a few moments now while working through your regret so that you can experience the fulfillment of Christ for the rest of your life? This battle of shame goes so far beyond motherhood, friends. But there is no better place to start fighting it than right here.

Shame is often one of the emotions that we try to conceal the most from others, including God. But it is also the release of this emotion that frees us the most when we bring it out of the darkness and into the light of his grace. Today I want you to take that deep shame that you have been hiding for so long and bring it before the Lord in prayer. If it's a sin that you haven't asked forgiveness for, this is your time. Trust in the truth that there is no sin, no shame too big for God to redeem. Give it all to him today, friend.

If you have already taken that step and have continued to hold on to the regret of your mistakes, it's time to lay it down at the foot of the cross again today. It will be painful to bring it back out from the depths of your heart, but, sweet mama, your heart is worth being rid of this hidden shame. This regret has held you back for far too long; it's too big of a burden for you to keep carrying by yourself. Let's release our regret together today and step into everything that God wants for our lives and our motherhood.

Dear God,

I have been holding on to this regret for far too long, and it is crippling me. Today I realize how much it is holding me back. God, I want to walk in your truth for my life, but I know that I can't take another step forward without giving this to you and allowing your grace to truly wash over my shame. Today I will let you break these chains of regret so that I can keep stepping forward into the future you have for me. When this regret comes back to my mind again, I ask that you would remind me of the truth I read in your Word today and that you would help me to forget what was behind and look to who you want me to become. In Jesus' name I pray,

Amen.

Day 29

WHEN MAMA SETS THE EXAMPLE

*Train yourself for godliness; for while bodily training is of some value,
godliness is of value in every way, as it holds promise for the present life
and also for the life to come . . . Let no one despise you for your youth,
but set the believers an example in speech, in conduct, in love, in faith,
in purity.*

1 TIMOTHY 4: 7–8, 12

"I'm a good person. I just want my kid to grow up to be a good person, too."

I think we've all said it at some point as a mom, right? But do you think that maybe we've done our kids and ourselves a disservice by only setting the standard at "good"? What if I told you that the standard of "good" isn't enough for God, and it shouldn't be enough for you, either? What if I told you that the baseline of "good" is too low?

But godliness . . . that's a different standard entirely, because it's a standard that sets the bar for you to *thrive*.

Remember earlier this month that we talked about living in the trap of unrealistic expectations, and how as moms we have the opportunity to set a tone of peace in our homes by where we place the bar? What we have to realize, mama, is that the bar isn't just meant to be set once, only for us to walk away and never have it be reassessed. No, it's meant to be revisited day after day, season after season, and set to the standard of holiness, to strive in being a *living example* of Jesus.

And what are we setting the bar in? Is it in the next big thing that the internet has to offer? The next "best" stroller, or clothing line, or swaddling blanket, or toy, or vacation? No. It's the bar set in our words and in our actions, in the way we love and in our faith and the purity of our hearts. *It's the bar set in the example of godliness through the gospel of Jesus Christ.*

I don't know about you, but I don't want to spend another minute of my motherhood setting an example for my children that isn't focused on eternity, friend. I don't want to waste another day staying trapped in the emotions of my heart and the darkness of my mind that gives my kids an example of anything other than godliness and what it has the power to do in their lives. The weight of our children's souls—it should weigh heavily on our hearts, mama. And like we talked about a few weeks ago, discipling our kids is the greatest responsibility we have as moms this side of heaven. But we must not take lightly that our example is crucial for our children.

Are you setting the example that godliness trumps surface-skimming goodness?

Are you setting the example that the condition of your heart is more important than the number on the tag of your shorts?

Are you setting the example that words of peace are more powerful than a tongue of anger?

Are you setting the example that being kind and good will not save them but that being redeemed by the kindness and goodness of the King when they didn't deserve it will?

And are you setting the example that emotions, when looked at through the lens of the gospel and transformed by the God who sent his Son to die for them, will be the only thing that will set them free?

Mama friend, we have this one shot, this one lifetime to influence our kids. While there is grace in the everyday, there is a consistent standard to be set. It isn't one set in fear or in shame or in insecurity, but set in godliness that you live out in front of your children in the everyday mundane.

Is it exhausting, yes. Is the transformation of our example painful at times? Yes. Are we going to fail? Yes. But are our kids and the call of the gospel in our lives worth setting the example for? *Absolutely.*

Take One Step into Peace:
Set a Godly Example

While it isn't our job to be the Holy Spirit to our children, it is our responsibility to point them to it. And the best way we can do that is in the example that we set. As we have walked through these emotions together over the last month, I want you take a look back and see where you have grown in your example. Go through the previous chapters and be reminded of where God has been working on your heart and meeting you in your brokenness. Has the example you are setting for your children changed this last month? Where are areas that you have seen God heal your heart? It can be so overwhelming to know the responsibility we have as moms to raise our children for Christ.

But when we look back and see God's goodness in our lives and how he has changed us for the better, it makes the road ahead seem less burdensome and more hope-filled. Today, "May the God of hope fill you with all joy and peace in believing, so that by the power of the Holy Spirit you may abound in hope" (Rom. 15:13).

Dear God,

What an incredible responsibility you have given me in setting an example of your love for my children. It can be so scary knowing that you have entrusted me with this, but I am confident that you will continue to help me set an example for my kids that honors you. Help me to be encouraged by how far you have already brought me in my journey of motherhood so that I can continue to look forward, knowing that you will keep working for my good and for the good of the hearts of my children. Help me to be bold in my example for them, teaching them all that you have taught me and for them to find their hope and peace in you. In Jesus' name I pray,

Amen.

Day 30

WHEN GOD LETS YOU WALK INTO THE FIRE

For freedom Christ has set us free; stand firm therefore, and do not submit again to a yoke of slavery.

GALATIANS 5:1

Something had been off for weeks. But it was more than off; everything was just wrong. *This just can't be happening to me,* I thought. *God, you cannot let this be. Where are you?* The weeks turned into months and it had only gotten worse.

The baby would cry, and it took everything in me to go and pick him up. I knew I was supposed to still feel tired, but to feel nothing? How could I not be feeling a thing? I began to experience resentment for my children and my husband. The very thought of going to church, let alone picking up my Bible and praising God, seemed inauthentic and forced. Instead, I found myself on my closet floor in tears.

Afraid of my own mind.

Alone in my sorrow.

Isolated in my loneliness.

Dulled by a fog that never seemed to lift.

Enslaved to my emotions and the lies of my mind.

And wondering why God ever would have let this happen to me.

I never thought that this would be a part of my story, especially as a woman of faith. But here I was, four months out from having our third baby and I was completely consumed by the darkness of postpartum depression and anxiety. It was crippling me from the inside out.

One of my very favorite stories from the Old Testament comes from the book of Daniel. It's the story of Shadrach, Meshach, and Abednego; it was my favorite Bible story as a kid. When the story takes place, Nebuchadnezzar was the king of Babylon. It was during his reign that he had a large idol made of gold and instructed all the people in his kingdom to bow down and worship it when the trumpets would sound through the city. All of the people obeyed. All but three.

Shadrach, Meshach, and Abednego would not bow down to the golden idol. Their obedience and praise belonged to the Lord, not to the king or his idol. When the king heard this, he gave the three Jewish men one last chance to bow down to the idol, or they would be thrown into the fiery furnace and burned alive. Even though they knew the consequences, Shadrach, Meshach, and Abednego held true to their convictions and would not bow to the golden idol, confident of their trust in God. Infuriated, King Nebuchadnezzar threw the three men into the fire. But what happened next, nobody could have expected. The furnace was opened to reveal not three but four men walking about in the midst of the fire, untouched by the flames; the three Jewish men and a man who looked like "a son of the gods" (Daniel 3:25).

Even though God had allowed them to be thrown into the fire, Jesus met them in its midst and allowed them to walk out of it.

I don't know about you, friend, but there have been a handful of times in my life when I have wondered why God has allowed me to go through excruciating pain, especially in motherhood. I have prayed and begged and petitioned and fasted over seasons of great brokenness in my life. Things that have brought me to the hottest places of the flames, places that have made me question whether or not God really does work all things together for my good. And yet, time and time again, God has allowed me to walk into the fiery furnace, *but he has always sent Jesus in to walk me out of it.*

I wish that you and I were sitting around my kitchen table with a piece of pie and a cup of coffee today. I wish that I could hold your hands and we could weep in our brokenness together. Oh, how I long to wipe the tears from your weary-mama face and hold you close like only sisters can. And if you were here, I would brush your three-days-unwashed hair back behind your ear and whisper, "And even though, he is sufficient."

Even though you lost your baby.

Even though your marriage is crumbling.

Even though motherhood was nothing like you thought it would be.

Even though you can't get pregnant.

Even though your child is sick.

Even though you have postpartum depression and anxiety.

Even though you wonder who you have become.

Even though you are more broken and more lost than you have ever felt and you don't feel like you can get out of bed another day, "My grace is sufficient for you, for my power is made perfect in weakness" (2 Cor. 12:9).

I wish that brokenness wasn't a part of my story; I wish it

wasn't a part of yours, either. I wish that there were seasons of my life that I could erase and emotions that I would never have to feel again. In my selfishness, I wish that I could fix it all on my own and simply hush away the tears like I do for my babies with the hum of a midnight lullaby. And I wish God didn't allow suffering in motherhood to be a part of my story.

But to wish that is to also wish that he isn't preparing me for something glorious for the sake of his Kingdom.

In John 13:7 Jesus says, "You don't understand now what I am doing, but someday you will" (NLT). He was talking about the coming of his death as he washed the feet of his disciples—he knew that the hour was near. And I can only imagine how they looked at one another in confusion as their Master did the servant's dirty work of washing their feet. But for Jesus, this was a sign of humility and of great love for his dear friends. But the act of love that he was about to do on the cross? In his humanness, he wanted the cup taken from him. But he continued on to act in obedience to his Father's will.

And his will included suffering.

In my own brokenness and pain in motherhood, it is crucial for me to look to the example of Jesus in his suffering, in his *obedience* to suffer for the salvation of mankind. And for me, it is to be my joy to suffer and endure in hope because Jesus did the same in his obedience in his death on the cross (Phil. 2:8). Some days, it doesn't make sense. I don't understand why this is part of my story. But as I have been reminded time and time again, he is preparing me for something more in the furnace and is already making a way for me to walk out of it.

Something that can be found only in the beauty of my broken story for the glory of his Kingdom.

While I can't possibly know the details of your story, I know the One who does. And it doesn't matter whether or not I know your pain, because I'm not the one whose strength is going to be made perfect in it. Maybe you have been reading through these chapters each day for the last month and you've been holding back the one thing that has been the most painful, the most debilitating, the most heartbreaking, and keeping it at an arm's reach away from the Savior. Because while you long to be released from your brokenness, the thought of actually letting it go is terrifying; it's become a part of you and you wonder how you will even go on without it. That's the power that these skewed emotions have on our hearts, friend. The longer we hold on to them, the more the enemy makes us believe that they are a part of our identity.

But today, something was different when you read this. Something seeped into the very depths of your soul and beckoned you to come back out into the light again.

Today is the day that you take the darkest emotion that has the tightest hold on your heart and release it to the Father. Today one of the broken pieces gets picked up and put into a place of redemption. And it starts on your knees.

The power of the physical act of surrender is one that we so often forget. But when we physically release our brokenness to the Father, our hearts more easily follow suit. As you begin your prayer today, find a spot on your floor and get on your knees before the Lord. Close your eyes, and start with your hands clenched in fists and allow yourself to *physically* release the brokenness that you have been hanging on to for far too long. Let the Spirit move within you. Let him break those rusty shackles. Let him take this cup from you, friend. Let him redeem your brokenness and turn it into something beautiful.

Dear God,

I come before you in a place of brokenness today. A place that I have held on to for too long. Lord, I am tired of hanging on to this pain; I am weary from being bound to it. Today, I release it to you. God, take this from me! In my weakness, may your strength be manifested and your plan for my life be revealed. I surrender to your will and I declare in power that I am no longer a slave to my suffering. In Jesus' name I pray,

Amen.

Day 31

WHEN MOTHERHOOD IS REDEEMED

I have been crucified with Christ. It is no longer I who live, but Christ who lives in me. And the life I now live in the flesh I live by faith in the Son of God, who loved me and gave himself for me.

GALATIANS 2:20

There I was again. Jesus found me on the living room floor, surrounded by sippy cups, neatly folded piles of dish towels, little princess underwear, and tiny toy cars. In a world of motherhood that was so messy, I was trying so desperately to keep it all together.

I had felt him closing in for years, much like you have this last month, pursuing me and pressing in. It was making me feel more convicted than I had ever felt, yet I experienced more peace than I had ever known. He was so close to breaking through, despite my trying to keep him at arm's length. I knew that if he got any closer it would require ultimate dependence upon him and real change, real transformation: from a selfish woman who kept a tally of all her sins and hid the scars of things from her past from everyone, from living in fear and always asking the what-ifs and never fully surrendering to his Truth.

But Jesus? He saw me there. He saw me in my pit of shame and the darkness of my emotions. So there on the floor of my living room he joined me; there was no denying the prodding of his voice: "Am I enough for you?" he whispered.

I tried to turn my face away. "Are you enough for me?" I shuddered. "I should be asking you that. Why do you still want me? I'm so bad, so dirty. I'll never be good enough!" I cried, looking at my piles of perfectly folded dish towels. Why was I still trying to hide behind them? Why was I still trying so hard to keep it all together?

"Am I enough for you?" he asked again. "Even if...will I still be enough?"

I didn't want to answer. I restraightened the towels.

"Even if this all went away. Your husband. Your kids. The house. Your life. Everything you're trying to hold together. What if it was just me and you and the glass cases in your mind. What if you had to fully trust me with them? Do you think my love is enough to redeem?"

I didn't know if I could let all of those things go. I couldn't figure out why he kept wanting me, pursuing me, after all these years. I had been building my own tiny kingdom and forgetting about his. How could he still love me so much when I had held him back for so long?

But because he's God, he knew my thoughts. He knew why I had been hesitating.

"Because I've loved you since the beginning, my child. And when I look at you there in your tiny kingdom, trying so hard to fix it all on your own, trying to push down the emotions you're so embarrassed of, I see only my Son on that cross. Your shame is gone. There's nothing you can do. It's only my grace I see."

"But what if I mess up? What if I let you down again? What if I start to fall away and my emotions take over again?" I couldn't even look up at him.

"I still will want you. The price I paid has made you worthy. Stop. Trying. So. Hard. Hand it all over to me."

But now apart from the law the righteousness of God has been made known, to which the Law and the Prophets testify. This righteousness is given through faith in Jesus Christ to all who believe. There is no difference between Jew and Gentile, for all have sinned and fall short of the glory of God, and all are justified freely by his grace through the redemption that came by Christ Jesus. ROMANS 3:21–24 NIV

I knocked my pile of towels down. They scattered all over the floor.

That was it. I decided that he was going to be enough. That was the day on my living room floor that my kingdom crumbled and his was raised, when I fell off my throne and I handed him the glass cases. Everything changed. That was the day I stopped trying so hard, the day the lavish love of Jesus, the gospel, wrecked me. The day my chains were broken; the day my motherhood was redeemed; the day I was set free.

Take One Step into Peace:
Empower Other Women

This has been the most beautiful month with you, friend. While we started out strangers, we have taken the step of obedience and walked through the hardest emotions of motherhood together. Choosing to trust that when we hand our hearts and our emotions over to the One who created us to experience them, our lives can be changed and our motherhood restored.

Look down and see the shackles of the lies of your mind loose around you, friend. No longer are you bound by them, but you've been set free to run in his worthiness! What an amazing God we serve!

But as you're running in this newfound freedom, can I ask you to take one last step into peace? Would you grab another weary mama by the hand and walk with her in this Truth through her own trenches? You have been discipled this month and your heart changed by the power of God's Word and the freedom of surrender. Won't you take the brave step of discipling another woman who needs it just as badly?

The fact is that if you just take this message and apply it to your own life and your own family, the power of this message stops there. The goal of this book is to not only equip you for your own walk through motherhood, but then to take the freedom of it to the mama next door, or the new mom at your playdate, or the woman in the cubicle next to you at work.

Women empowering women through the transforming love of Jesus changes everything. And God is calling you to be that woman who empowers those around her today.

Dear God,

I thank you that you have met me in the messiness of motherhood this month and freed me from some of the hardest emotions I have ever felt. You are a powerful, loving God and I am living proof that trusting you with my emotions changes everything. God, I ask that you would give me boldness to walk with another mama through this book. Help me to have the courage and bravery to reach out, even if it makes me scared. I know the life-changing power of your love in motherhood, and I want to be able to help another mama find that, too. Thank you for taking my emotions and transforming them into something beautiful. Thank you for my redemption through Jesus' death and resurrection. And thank you for redeeming my motherhood. In Jesus' name I pray,

Amen.

ACKNOWLEDGMENTS

If there is one thing that I am sure of in this life, it is that I am nothing without the love of God. When I stand in front of the mirror and see the tired mama looking back at me, it is only his grace and mercy that I see. The unmerited forgiveness that the Father has poured out over my soul is the thing that I cherish the most in my life, yet will never fully comprehend. Thank you, Jesus, for saving me from myself. Thank you, Spirit, for giving me the words to write this book and the tools to bring the hope of the gospel to the mamas of the world.

God, may you receive all the glory and all the praise for the songs of my midnight lullabies. You alone are worthy.

It has been said that it takes a village to raise a child. It turns out it also takes a village to write a book. And the village begins with the parents. Thank you to my mom and dad—Rod and Lynda Janzen—for living a life in hard pursuit of the gospel, even when no one was looking. You both made Jesus real to me, and I will never have the words to tell you how much I love you or how much you have impacted my life.

When God created me, I believe that he did it with another person in mind. Eric, it is my greatest joy to be your wife. I continue to stand back in awe at how recklessly you love God and push me toward him daily. Even when I was in the deepest pit, you climbed down into it with me and led me back up while reminding me who I was in Christ. You never pushed. You never pulled. You led. You always lead in love. And you love me and the kids so well.

I also believe that when God created me, he had a plan for the little people I would bring into this world. My farm babies, Nora, Andi, and Deacon: you are our greatest, wildest adventure yet, and I don't think that's going to change anytime soon. You have taught me more as your mommy than I ever thought possible, and it's because of you that I have the honor of being a parent. I am so glad that God chose me to be part of your stories.

I didn't know how much love I could experience from my in-laws—Kim and Sheila Eberspacher. Your acceptance of my city-girl heart and flair for the exuberant has meant more to me than you know. Thank you for raising a son who loves God above everything else and modeling it in your own lives. I would not be who I am without you.

To Leslie Means: you took a chance on me at Her View From Home and gave me a place to share my heart. Not only have you mentored me for the last three years and poured into my career, you have become one of my very dearest friends. I am so thankful for you.

To Eryn Lynum: I'm so glad that we ran into one another in the hallway at the HACWN Conference. You were so gracious to impart your wisdom upon me, and I will be forever grateful that I met you and for our friendship.

To Les Stobbe: you saw something in me that October day in Kansas City and decided to listen to my story further. I am so grateful that you sought me out and that you became my agent, even if for just a short time. But even in your leaving the industry, you left me in the hands of the best agent to take the reins. Bob Hostetler, you have been nothing short of a Godsend to me and my career. Time and time again, you have given me such wisdom and guided me through this entire process. I am so thankful that God led me to you.

To Keren Baltzer and the entire team at FaithWords: you have taken a woman who is green to the publishing world and walked very faithfully down this road with me. You have taken my dream of *Midnight Lullabies* and turned it into reality. Thank you for all of the precious time that you have spent seeing my vision and running after it with me.

To my girls, Allison, Jill, Brittany, and Megan: thank you for being the most faithful friends. When a girl prays for community, you are who she longs for. I love growing in Christ with each of you, and I am blown away how much you have rallied around me and this book. I'm thankful you are my people.

And to my readers of From Blacktop to Dirt Road and the readers of *Midnight Lullabies*: there is no way that I can end this without acknowledging you. When I wrote this devotional, I had you in mind, you and your precious hearts. There was not one word that wasn't intentionally written for you, and my desire is for you to have your motherhood changed by the power of the gospel. Thank you for reading my words, and thank you for your years of readership and commitment to make From Blacktop to Dirt Road a gospel-centered community for the everyday woman to experience redemption and joy. May your midnight lullabies be filled with it.

INDEX

A

anger, taking a stand against,
33–36, 46–50

B

becoming more, taking a stand for,
1–5
Bible study, small groups at church
and, 98–100
Bible verses. *See* scripture verses
big girl panties, lie of, 2–3
body (yours)
becoming an idol, 51–54
overcoming insecurities about,
54–55, 105–108
bride, forgetting how to be, 113–117
brokenness, letting Him redeem,
140–142

C

church
connecting at, small groups and,
97–100
feeling defeated at, 96–100
getting plugged in, 98–100
transcending boundaries of the
building, 98
cleaning, taking a break from,
92–95
comparisons, dealing
with, 55–60

conversations, initiating, 85–86
cookies, baking, handling demands
like, 37–41

D

decisions, wisdom for, 42–45
demands, handling, 37–41
discipleship, obedience, mentors
and, 87–91
disciples, leading children to
become, 11, 72–76, 88, 98
disciplining kids, parenting with
shame and, 122–126

E

emotions
God's peace and, xiv–xv
as indicators, not dictators, xiv
overwhelming, identity crisis and,
xiii–xiv
pushing down, the lie of, 2–3
reclaiming by taking a stand
against, xv–xvi
reconciling hurt feelings,
101–104
surrendering to the Lord, 4–5
trapped by, xiv
empowering other women, 145–147
the enemy, lies of
awareness of raw emotions and,
xiii–xiv

the enemy, lies of (*Contd.*)
   pushing down/compartmentaliz-
      ing emotions, 3–5
   standing up against, xv–xvi. *See also*
      taking a stand
   telling you you're not enough,
      6–9
example, setting for your children,
   131–135
expectations, when not
      met, 24–28

F

fear
   attacking, 69–71
   consuming you, 66–71
feelings. *See* emotions
fire, when God lets you walk into,
   136–142
forgiveness, for shaming children,
   125–126
friends and friendship
   initiating conversations and,
      85–86
   practicing friendship with God,
      18–19
   reconciling hurt feelings,
      101–104
   when pride holds you back,
      82–86
   when you still want a friend,
      20–23

G

gift, motherhood becoming yours,
   109–112
God
   asking for strength of, 120–121
   Jesus Christ and. *See* Jesus Christ
   letting you walk into the fire,
      136–142
   peace of, reclaiming emotions
      and, xiv–xvi
   practicing friendship with, 18–19
   setting example for, 133–135

H

housecleaning, perspective on,
   92–95
humbling ourselves, 82–86
hurt feelings, reconciling, 101–104
husband
   anger, resentment and, 46–50
   being a bride to, 113–117
   being a witness to, 99
   getting lost in parenthood with,
      114
   having vulnerable conversation
      with, 79–81
   investing in, 115–117
   seasons of sacrifice and, 77–81
   sex life, prayer life and, 29–32

I

idol, golden, 137
idol, when mom bod becomes,
   51–54
illness, dealing with, 118–121

J

Jesus Christ. *See also* God
   being living example of, 131–135
   chasing after character of, 103
   commanding us to make
      disciples, 72–76
   effects of trusting in, 57
   empowerment through, 7
   looking at emotions through lens
      of, 4
   making decisions to honor, 123
   mistakes, regret, forgiveness and,
      128–129

overcoming fear through, 68–69

peace and joy of, through truth and trusting in God and, 63, 68–69, 120

pointing children to, raising families in, 11, 72–76, 88, 98

redemption of motherhood and, 143–147

scriptural references. *See* scripture verses

security from and keeping eyes on, 26, 56–59

Shadrach, Meshach, Abednego and, 137

speaking name to children, 11

suffering of, your suffering and, 139

validating/empowering other women in, 111

when God lets you walk into the fire and, 136–142

joy

    return of, following depression, 61–65

    of truth and trusting in God/Christ, 63, 68–69, 120

L

lists, making and managing demands, 39–41

loneliness, taking stand against, 15–19, 80

M

mentor, finding, 89–91

motherhood

    as act of worship, 11–13

    becoming your gift, 109–112

    darkness of, 6–9, 62–63, 132

    emotions of. *See* emotions

    redemption of, 143–147

taking a stand for emotions and. *See* taking a stand

O

offering (sacred), bringing, 8–14

P

pain, when God lets you walk into the fire of, 136–142

parenting with shame, 122–126

peace

    of God, reclaiming your emotions and, xiv–xvi

    taking steps to. *See* taking one step into peace

perfectionism, perspectives on, 23–24, 25–26, 92–94

playing with your kids, 105–108

postpartum depression, 61–62, 137, 138

potty training, expectations and, 24–28

prayers, by topic. *See* taking one step into peace

pride, humbling, 82–86

R

reconciliation, seeking, 102–104

redemption of motherhood, 143–147

regret, dealing with and releasing, 127–130

resentment, eliminating, 46–50

S

sacrifice, seasons of, 77–81

scripture verses

    Acts 2:46–47, 96

    1 Corinthians 6:19, 51

    1 Corinthians 10:23, 37

    2 Corinthians 12:9, 138

scripture verses (*Contd.*)

2 Corinthians 10:3–5, 55

Daniel 3:25, 137

Ephesians 4:31–32, 101

Ephesians 5:1– 2, 12

Galatians 2:20, 143

Galatians 5:1, 1, 136

Hebrews 10:24–25, 98

Isaiah 26: 3–4, xvi

James 1:5–6, 42

James 1:19–20, 34

1 John 5:14, 29

John 10:10, 4

John 13:7, 139

John 16:33, 66, 68

Luke 6:36, 92

Mark 10:6–9, 113

Matthew 6:25, 105

Matthew 28:19–20, 72

Micah 7:7, 24

1 Peter 2: 9, 6

1 Peter 3:1, 99

1 Peter 4:10–11, 109

Philippians 2:8, 139

Philippians 3:12–14, 127

Philippians 4:6, 31

Philippians 4:7, 103

Proverbs 15:1, 33

Proverbs 17:17, 82

Proverbs 31:11, 77

Psalm 16:5, 18

Psalm 34:4–5, 51

Psalm 46:1–3, 118

Psalm 103:8–12, 122

Psalm 139:13–14, 20

Romans 3:21–24, 145

Romans 12:1–2, 10

Romans 15:13, 61, 63, 134

1 Timothy 4:7–8, 12, 131

2Timothy 1:7, 8

Titus 2:3–5, 87

self-care, practicing, 64–65

self-sufficiency, false sense of, 84, 89

setting the example for your children, 131–135

sex life, prayer life and, 29–32

Shadrach, Meshach, and Abednego, story of, 137

shame, parenting with, 122–126. *See also* regret

sickness, dealing with, 118–121

strength of God, asking for, 120–121

swimming pool, overcoming body insecurities and, 105–108

T

taking a stand

about: events leading to lullabies for, xiii; reclaiming emotions by, xv–xvi

against anger, 33–36, 46–50

against anxiety of time demands, 37–41

to become more (and the lie of big-girl panties), 1–5

against loneliness, 15–19, 80

offering gift of motherhood to God, 10–14

against perfectionism (taking a break from cleaning), 92–95

in seasons of sacrifice, 77–81

setting the example for your children, 131–135

when comparisons show up, 55–60

when enemy tells you you're not enough, 6–9

when expectations aren't met, 24–28

when fear is consuming, 66–71

when feeling defeated at church,
96–100

when getting feelings hurt,
101–104

when getting sick, 118–121

when given a choice to play with
kids, 105–108

when God lets you walk into the
fire, 136–142

when Jesus commands us to make
disciples, 72–76

when mama gets her joy back,
61–65

when motherhood becomes your
gift, 109–112

when motherhood is redeemed,
143–147

when pride holds you back,
82–86

when regret rules you,
127–130

when sex life meets prayer life,
29–32

when wisdom is needed, 42–45

when you forget how to be a
bride, 113–117

when you parent with shame,
122–126

when you're asked to pay a price,
87–91

when your mom bod becomes an
idol, 51–54

when you still want a friend,
20–23

taking one step into peace (and
prayer for)

asking for God's strength,
120–121

asking for wisdom, 44–45

breaking bondage of comparison,
58–60

declaring that you belong to
Him, 8–9

empowering other women,
145–147

entering into touchy situations,
35–36

finding a mentor for
discipleship, 89–91

getting plugged in at church,
98–100

having vulnerable conversation
with husband, 79–81

initiating conversations, 85–86

investing in your husband,
115–117

knocking down idols, 53–54

laying down expectations, 26–28

leaving one thing undone today,
94–95

letting go of anger/resentment,
35–36, 48–50

letting Him redeem your
brokenness, 140–142

making lists to manage demands,
39–41

playing with your kids today,
107–108

practicing friendship with God,
18–19

practicing self-care, 64–65

praying for future friends,
22–23

praying into our sex lives, 31–32

praying the Gospel over your
kids, 75–76

putting up a memorial (sacred
offering), 12–14

reconciling hurt feelings,
102–104

releasing regret and shame,
129–130

taking one step (*Contd.*)
  seeking forgiveness for shaming
    children, 125–126
  setting Godly example, 133–135
  surrendering your emotions, 4–5
  validating others, 111–112

V
validating others, 111–112

W
wisdom, needing, 42–45
women, empowering, 145–147

ABOUT THE AUTHOR

LAUREN EBERSPACHER is a blogger and author, living intentionally for Jesus, with a desire to give heartfelt encouragement to the everyday mama and wife. At her blog, From Blacktop to Dirt Road (fromblacktoptodirtroad.com), she writes about all things faith, farm, and old-fashioned homemaking, sharing real-life moments with a healthy dose of laughter along the way.

She is a stay-at-home mom to her three small children and a learn-in-progress farm wife to her bearded farmer, Eric. They live in Milford, Nebraska.